Echoes
Of My Time

Echoes
Of My Time

Anne Bardsley

To order additional copies of this book, contact:
Xlibris Corporation
0-800-644-6988
www.xlibrispublishing.co.uk
Orders@xlibrispublishing.co.uk
304790

CONTENTS

I SHOUDN'T BE ALIVE BUT I AM
Learn from yesterday live for today and hope for tomorrow

ONE WOMANS STORY OF
CHILDHOOD ABUSE IN
CHILDCARE SERVICES
AND ABUSES WITHIN
PSYCHIATRIC HOSPITALS

CHAPTER 1

The reunion

The distance was long, not only in time and miles but also in years. Forty—nine years to be exact. That is how long we had been parted, but today all that was going to change. I was meeting my eldest sister Margaret, who live in Canada, for the very first time. As the plane was descending to land I was getting both very nervous and excited at the forth-coming meeting. Unfortunately, for my fellow passengers this meant that I was talking nonstop broad Glaswegian and they had no escape from my continual nervous chattering from Glasgow International Airport to Toronto International Airport. I literally had a captive audience and I am sure they must have been as glad to see the back of me and feel very sorry for the poor sister who was going to have to put up with me.

There were a few coincidences that day that added to the excitement and magic of the moment. While I was telling anybody who would listen to my news, especially the lady in the second seat, in the same row as me who seemed equally as excited for me. While her husband was waiting for the plane to land to meet her, my sister and her partner were doing the same thing waiting for me. Now you are probably asking yourself what so special about that? Nothing really, until you realise the woman I was talking to was the wife of the man my sister was talking to and he was being told the same story told to him by my sister. An Oprah Winfrey moment or what! How did I find this out, again by coincidence? As I was waiting for wheelchair assistance to get me off the plane, this meant that I was going to be in the last few off the plane. So I had said to this woman, who had had to put up with me the whole journey from Glasgow to Toronto

"If you see a wee woman with gingery hair, could you tell her that her sister is still on the plane but will be one of the last off and could she still wait on me. I hadn't missed the flight or changed my mind about coming"?

I garbled desperately as quicker and quicker as the plane emptied until I was the only one left, me waiting for wheelchair assistance and a person being arrested for something. I remember two things very clearly even in my heightened state of excitement. I hoped that the lady would find Marge and I thought that the policeman on board was a real hunk and maybe I would just stay in Canada and find me a nice handsome Mountie husband. Getting back to the lady, thanks to that lady who did a total stranger a good turn when she could have just walked out of the airport terminal, amazingly she met her husband talking to my sister and passed on the message. I don't remember the lady's name, but if you were the poor demented soul sitting next to a ranting Scottish lass then I would like to take the opportunity to thank you from the bottom of my heart. Due to you passing on the message we did meet that day, and we hugged and cried and hugged some more, neither one of us wanting to be the first to break the hug, afraid that it might all dissolve into a dream. But it really was reality; we were finally together through obstacles and miracles, what are the chances of a stranger finding "A wee woman with gingery hair", especially at an International Airport. The probability is likely to be infinite. The other thing I clearly remember was

"Oh my god that policeman was an absolute hunk, and if all Canadian men looked like him, then maybe I'll just stay here and find a nice Canadian man to settle down with and not bother going home"

Nevertheless, here I was In Canada for the first time in my life and I can assure you it will not be my last (I have since been to Canada three more times). However, how had it come to this and why had it taken so long to track each other down.

Let me take you Back forty-nine years to the year 1960, it was the year that was to change our lives, my elder sister Graces', my sister Marge and mine.

CHAPTER 2

The early years

There were originally three sisters who were split up as babies and the two who went into care did not know of the third sister for 49years. My elder sister Grace and I were sent into the "care system", while Marge was adopted by an Aunt and Uncle. When Marge was seven the family immigrated to Canada, the strangest part of all was at some points in our young lives we were only as far away as three miles away from each other and we did not even know it.

This is the youngest sisters' story.

The year is 1960, although not the year I was born which was 1959. I was the youngest of three sisters. My biological mother and father I have no recollection of, and I may have this part of the story wrong because my memory lets me down at times, and I only know what I have been told and seen in pictures. My mother was called Winifred McCallum and my Father was called Patrick Cronin Currie. This I knew through my birth certificate. Although I was named after my mother, Winifred, a name which I always hated, and which at times was shortened to Freda which I hated even more I had no pictures of them or of what they looked like, or at least my mother looked like, until three years ago (2007) after my last foster mum, or at least the person I considered to be my mum, Mary Ritchie, Died at the age of 93 after a stroke. To me she was the one I put through heartbreak and hell with my wild ways, tears and tantrums., She was the one there when I was a child to wipe my tears, put a plaster on yet another skinned knee and there to teach me right from wrong and to love me. In addition, and to me importantly be the first adult I gradually trusted and loved back, to the day she died. Even today, when I think about her and how my own circumstances now almost mirror hers but I am only fifty three years old, I can so much more appreciate her mind set in her later years. I say this not of out of self-pity, or for all of my ailments but out of an understanding and appreciation of what she felt in her later years. However, I am the lucky One. Yes I now have more problems than I ever did before but it just makes me realise what a strong person my mother was, and how much I still miss her and how much she taught me. I believe that through various signs she is giving me that strength through Angels. Another coincidence Marge also believes in Angels. I also believe in Karma and what harm or hurt you did to others will follow you and find a way of payback time in whatever shape or form that it takes. I firmly believe that I am now in payback time, through all the illness I now have. Yes Karma will always catch up with you. I also believe Mother Nature is fighting back because of all the damage that we, as humans, have done. However that is another story for another day. Getting back to my story, all I know of my biological parents are that they both liked to drink and both remarried after they split from the original marriage, which produced us three original sisters. Through reading the local paper's hatches matches and dispatches or to those of you unused to the term, the births marriages and deaths, we found that my biological father went on to re marry and have three sons. The reason we know this is on his death notice it mentioned three sons names. Strangely my biological mother did the same, but she had three daughters. Now I don't mean to be bitter but you can't help thinking did they ever think about their first three daughters? I know my father did because what I do know is that at some point in his life my dad had asked about us and asked the rest of the family relatives to look out for us and if we ever came back to the area to open their door to us. Give them their due they did, for a short while anyway. But after about a year it sort of ran its course and we all once again went our own ways. I also remember that my mother had asked to see us round about 1975 but was denied the opportunity by the social work department, saying that she had given up her right to see us by abandoning us years earlier. I was actually devastated by this news, as it had been the opportunity that I had been waiting for. There were so many questions that I wanted to ask her, like why had she given us up in the first place? Was she unable to cope with three young babies? Or were there other reasons she gave us up. I did not feel bitter towards her I just wanted to know the reason why, because I believe that a mother does not give up her children for nothing. Now the social workers in their own weird and wonderful ways had made sure that we never met. And that only added to my hatred of social workers good or bad. In my young eyes all they ever did was take you away from the family you found yourself in with no thought too how you felt or explained why you were moving yet again. However I can only commend my Aunt Margaret who, along with her own family had taken us into her home and gave us all, Margaret, Grace and me a home for as long as she could manage. When I caught up with my Aunt Margaret in Canada she was telling me that she had looked after us all for nine months. She told me this funny story. There were times when she would put me out in the garden in my pram, which you did in those days, and unbeknown to my Aunt Margaret, my mother would come back from the pub and take me home to her house without telling my Aunt Margaret. When my Aunt Margaret went outside to bring me back in I was gone. This as you can imagine put my Aunt Margaret in a spin and panic until she realized that my mother in her drunken stupor had taken me once again and Aunt Margaret would trundle round to my mother and get me back and leave my mother to sober up again and nurse yet another hangover. My Aunt Margaret kept us for as long as she could cope, which unfortunately was for only nine months but she did it none the less and I take my hat off to her as she was then left with the agonizing decision to send us back to our parents. It must be mentioned at this point that my mother had scarpered off out of the marriage and our lives and my father was left to cope on his own. Unfortunately he ended up in prison for whatever reason I don't know and never will, so once again it was back to Aunt Margaret's'. But this time the outcome was to be very different. Margaret the eldest sister was adopted by my Aunt Margaret and my Aunt had to make the heart-breaking decision to put Grace and me into the care of the social work system. If she knew of the horrors that lay ahead of us both I believe she would have tried somehow to keep the family together. Sadly that was not to be, and I often wonder how differently my life would have been. I found out about Margaret (Marge) as she likes to be called, from my sister Grace who is the middle sister. After our foster mum, Mary Ritchie, died, Grace gave me the letters and photos that Marge had send her from the three previous years. I had somehow always known I had an older sister who was adopted and taken to Canada and it was always my goal and drive that I would meet her before I died. Don't get me wrong I have absolutely no intentions of dying yet but I was annoyed that Grace had not told me sooner about marge because as a Child or teenager or whatever age I was I always had this "notion", or knowledge or buried memory of someone telling me or through intuition or call it a gut feeling that I had a big sister, no matter what I thought of was true, I was never really sure if this was my imagination or if it was true, so when Grace confirmed the facts for me I was delighted. But something stranger than science fiction took place when I wrote my book My Journey to Freedom and had a launch for it, it was there that I met my step brother and cousin and his wife. Now this might sound confusing but he is one of the same people. Jim is my step-brother because he is Marge's adopted brother, she is my sister but he is also my cousin because he is my Aunt Margaret's son. At the launch he said that he could find Marge for me I had the whole place in tears, James and Shirley who were the cousins, were also in tears and there and then I made a decision, I was somehow going to Canada to meet with Margaret if she would have and accept me. Now you may be wondering why I thought that Marge may not accept me? The reason is quite simple I have serious mental health problems and so far many of my newfound relatives have shied away from me and the relationship between Grace and me because of it has not blossomed as either me or my mother wanted but that's life and you move on. It does surprise me a bit about Grace and my relationship given that we were both in the care system at the same time and although I cannot speak for Grace, for me, it was the worst possible time in my life. We were both sent from foster home to children's home to foster home to children's home and by the time I was five we had been moved approximately twenty times. It was then that I decided my name was not going to be Winifred Currie or McLean or Young or Gallagher or whatever any other family wanted to call me. At the Grand old age of five I decided that my name was Anne and Grace's name was Susan, however Grace was having none of it her name was Grace and Grace it was staying.

But what was so wrong with this "Care System" that a five year old wanted to change her name and become unidentifiable or more to the point invisible. With over twenty moves in five short years moving to various children's homes and foster families from Scotland to England and back to Scotland it begged the question why were Grace and me moved so often within the first five and six years of our young lives?. Why? Especially as it is well documented that the first five years of any child's life are what will shape them as adults. However in our case the answer was apparently glaringly simple. People wanted to believe all that we were accused of was true, because it was written in our "MISSING CASE FILES (the reason I emphasized the lost or missing case files is that they were found, by another social worker at a much later time in my life which was while I was detained in a maximum security psychiatric hospital.) However any time my foster mum wanted to look at them this was the excuse she was always given by our social worker at that time, the early nineteen sixties. The social worker we had at that time also believed "we couldn't be house trained" their reasoning for this was because I was a persistent bed wetter and pants wetter and would just sit rocking back and forth not saying much of anything at all. Why? because I was traumatised by previous continuous abuse, which was always followed by yet another move to yet one more children's home or foster home and family with its' own level of abuse and terror and ruled by fear. But did anybody ask why? No! Between this and being labelled backward, stupid, disturbed, maladjusted and various other adjectives and names the social worker decided to call us this was why we were moved so often. Apparently, according to our foster mum, when she took us out of one of the children's homes, we did not even know, how to play and no one ever thought to ask me why I sat there rocking, just rocking back and forth, back and forth, with my tongue rolling round my mouth until I had a large vicious red ring round my mouth making me look like a clown. Talking about clowns, I remember meeting the famous Co-Co the clown at a fete in Somerset England while we were staying with yet another foster family who lived in Wellyngarden City which were actually very nice to us. However at this fair this Co-Co the clown squeezed my hand so tightly I thought that he had broken my fingers. Don't adults realize that a child's hand is not only much smaller but also much more delicate too. Getting back to the fete What I also remember vividly from that day out at the fete was that I was put on a pony backwards and then some sick person slapped the pony's rump and off it trotted with me hanging onto its' tail for dear life screaming, but nobody took my screams on, they just laughed as only adults do when they think silly or dangerous thing happen until as you would expect I finally fell off. After I fell off amazingly none the worse, only shook up a bit, the adults came running realizing it wasn't so funny after all. This left me with an inbuilt fear and dread of horses. How surprising! However I did, years later work with horses at Silverknowes Riding for the Disabled with adults with learning difficulties which I absolutely adored. Our "Dad" at the time was a travelling salesman and although he went all over the world, he always found time to bring us both back a doll in National costume from wherever he had been. One of my favourite dolls that my "daddy brought me back from his travels" was a little black doll whose eyes were in 3D when you moved her or when you turned her upside down. Another thing I remember from this family was that they had an orchard of apples and grew their own vegetables including marrow which I hated. I have a fond memory of picking up apples that had fallen to the ground and placing them in the round space hollowed out from the green and purple cardboard trays before going off to market. I remember every week day before going to bed we would watch Florence and the Magic Roundabout and on Saturdays we would watch Dr Who and then scare ourselves silly with the "Daleks" not to mention the opening tunnel sequence which actually felt like it was pulling you into the tunnel and you would drown. We always had sausage chips and spaghetti on a Saturday night and every Saturday night after going to bed I would be as sick as a parrot on the spaghetti. This became a Saturday ritual because the more I said I didn't like spaghetti the more I was given it the more I would be sick. This would continue until the message finally got through to that particular set of foster parents that I really did not like spaghetti. One of my favourite chores that I was asked to do and it in no way could be called a chore was peeling the pea pods, "two to the basket with the hole and five too me" I loved this and all the lovely new peas, that was until I had a sore tummy and when asked if I had eaten any of the peas I would sit there tears running down my face and pleaded not to be beaten. At this statement my mummy at that time put her arms around me, gently wiped my tears from my face and gave me a promise that she would never ever give me a beating. The family in England were one of the nicest families we were with. While in England I started school at Saint Pauls. Before we went to school and after breakfast we would go to church at eight o'clock in the morning for morning prayers after that we would make our way to school. I remember Saint Pauls Primary affectionately as it was one of the first schools that I started in along with Cardross Park primary and Knoxland primary. It soon became quite clear early on that I was a bit of a clumsy child. I was always falling over my own feet or out of some tree I had just climbed or fence I thought that I was able enough to jump or swing over. One of my brilliant ideas was of trying to ride a three wheeled bike called a tricycle, not surprisingly it ended in disaster when I couldn't find the brakes, I went head first over the handle bars, landed in a stingy nettle bush and was covered in stings. As you might expect I was screaming with the pain and at around four years of age, I didn't have the knowledge to find docken leaves.

Another place we were sent to while very young, we must have been three and four going on four and five, was a farm on the north of Scotland. I do not remember my exact age but I do know that I had not started school and attend what was called a kindergarten. What I do remember was that I did not know what a kindergarten was. In todays' language, it is now commonly known as a nursery. Every day we walked the three miles there and at the end of the day, we walked those same three miles back. What I also remember, as I am sure many young children will, remember was the bright red sore ring that your black rubber unlined waterproof wellington boots left because your socks had fallen down. I remember this vividly as I had an almost permanent red sore ring round my legs because in the early sixties many families could not afford to buy you both shoes and wellingtons, so it was the cheapest option, the black wellington boots. The family on this farm seemed to be O.K. That was until I had chicken pox and was laid up in a big double bed that Grace and I shared. There I was bored at being stuck in bed covered in spots that itched so much I had some of the spots bleeding, but that was not what got me into trouble. What really got me into trouble was when I got up; found an empty bottle of the little cream jars you used to get. Inside the lid of this small glass jar it had a rubber suction ring inside it. I remember breaking this ring into little pieces which was very easily done as it was very soft and was easily stretched and broken. Well what happened next I could not understand! You would have thought I had killed something instead of just breaking up a rubber ring. My "father" at the time dragged me out of bed lifted up my nightie and leathered my legs and buttocks with a two tong brown leather belt. My punishment didn't stop there. I was dragged to the hay shed which had haystacks in it and before I had the chance to even start screaming my "father" had lifted me up on a ladder and dropped me roughly on top of the haystack. He then took the ladder away and I started to scream. His gruff response was that I could scream away to my hearts' content as nobody was going to hear me. He kept me there until the next morning in among the mice the rats and whatever other creepy crawlies you get in a haystack and farm barn. Grace God love her, tried to give me food but it was impossible, she was as small as me and could not lift the ladders, but God bless you Grace you tried to help your little sister at your own risk of being caught and punished in a similar way or worse.

Going back to the social worker, and the terms that they used to describe us, of not being able to be house trained which was why we were moved so often according to them, now my idea of not being able to be house trained would usually only apply to animals, so I could only assume that is the meaning that the authorities thought about us in we were no better than an animals. As much as I tried not to think about it, I could not help but think it was all because of me in particular due to the bed wetting and continual rocking.

I actually feel for the remaining relatives which made what must have been an agonizing decision to put us into care thinking that we would be well looked after and that at that time they had made the right decision. That decision changed our lives in ways that I still find hard to describe and for people to comprehend. And for me to have survived, as the examples I have recalled. Sometimes when I recall my childhood I actually feel lucky, having read what you have so far, oh yes there's more to come, you must be thinking how on earth can I possibly consider myself lucky. This is why. I was rescued out of the system. However, by the time my last foster mother got us back we didn't even know how to play, even with each other, but we were still lucky. Many didn't survive or get rescued. Maybe by reading my story and others (the children of the 1950's and 1960's) we will somehow find the recourse to justice and find ways to protect the children in today's care system.

I don't remember my first couple of years in care, I was only a baby. My first memory however is not a good one and even today when I hear that the same thing has happened to a child the same age as I was I am reliving the moment. I can, even after all these years still see feel, smell, and hear the incident that put me, my mind and my body into shock so much that I never spoke a word for six months, I just sat there rocking back and forth, my tongue going in and out in symmetry with my continual rocking. Why was my behaviour like this? Had I caused it? Or was I just a naughty attention-seeking three year? What am I talking about? I am talking about the rape of a three year old girl! And this was all because she wet her pants. A high price to pay for wet pants, but more importantly it should never have taken place. The rape of a child of any age is totally unacceptable. The sad thing is it still occurs even in todays' so called, tolerant society. I remember the rape like it was yesterday. Except when I was three years old, I did not know what was happening to me except that it was excruciatingly painful and started out as a game. But it is only as you get older does the enormity of the crime hit you, by which time you have blamed yourself and have no self-worth left because of it, unless you actually get professional help, you go through life with a total mistrust in men and no self-respect for yourself, and are unable to make relationships with men. This is what happened.

I lived with a family in Lossimouth, a small fishing village in the north—east coast of Scotland. I discovered to my delight that I had a brother a mummy and a daddy and a beloved granddad. I loved it here I went to visit my Granddad every Sunday. In the early 1960's it was normal to get dressed in your good clothes if you were going visiting, even if it was to another member of the family. So every Sunday I would put on a nice clean dress and visit my granddad. Now one of the reasons I loved to visit my grand dad was because he had rabbits and he would let me hold them and stroke them, that, and the fact that he used to always have a wee bag of sweets for me. I had a very close bond to my granddad. He told me that you don't pick rabbits up by their ears, as this would cause them pain. He always demonstrated this to me by loosely pinching my ears. I never saw this as a punishment but a lesson on how to look after my granddad's loved rabbits. The strange thing was grace never came with me to visit this Granddad, so where she went on a Sunday with our "mummy" I never really knew.

My Granddad was a lovely man. He always wore a fawn or beige (as It's now known) cardigan with leather elbow patches and a cloth cap. He loved his rabbits and I loved him and the rabbits not to mention the wee bag of sweets. But the day I wet my pants I never saw my beloved granddad again. Not because he died, but because we were once more taken away because I had wet my pants and kept my brother's secret promise

I was getting ready to go and see my granddad and had only my black patent button shoes to fasten, not a problem you might think! except that I was so desperate for the toilet that I couldn't concentrate to fasten my shoes. I kept saying that I needed but we must have been running late for a bus or something and my mummy insisted that I fasten my shoes first then I would get to the toilet. However, my bladder let me down and I not only wet my pants but my good dress and the flooring. So as a punishment, I was left behind for my brother to "see" to me. Which to most people in Scotland at that time meant washing me and changing my clothes and putting me in clean, dry ones? It did not quite turn out like that.

It was innocent enough at the start in that my brother who would have been about seventeen to nineteen years old and hormonal, or at least looking back he seemed to be about that age but to a three year old anybody who is over the age of ten is old, so I don't really have an accurate age gauge to go on. He took my clothes off then he took his own off. Being a child, I saw no harm to this except that I had never seen a penis or pubic hair before and did not know why he had one and I did not. At first it was a game and he asked me to hit it, I thought this was great fun, you hit this thing and it bounced and got bigger and the more I hit it the bigger it got until it was bulging and straight, I was laughing away quite happily in my innocence unaware that the next hour was going to be one of my most harrowing experiences of my life and would cause me to be traumatised for years. This is what happened next.

My brother asked me "do you want to see what this does ", and as curious as the next child I nodded in delight, This is our secret just you and I know about this, you have not to let anybody know, you need to promise not to tell anybody or the bad man will come and take you away. I understood I just knew that I was about to become part of a secret with my brother and that made me feel very special because I had missed out on seeing my granddad. Then However he showed me the real purpose of a penis and I remember thinking that I was going to choke or that this toy I had been playing with just a few moment earlier was tearing up my insides I screamed or at least tried to scream but my brother just covered my mouth and I did not feel so special when he lifted me up and just kept on ramming his manhood into my tiny fragile broken body. After that I thought my ordeal was over however he then ran a scalding hot disinfected, bleach bath the pain was indescribable until I passed out and then he took me back to the bedroom and changed the bed and me. I never told a soul but still I was taken away for more bad things to happen to me just like he said they would, and they did. But I never wanted to see my brother again as long as I lived but the damage was done. I had been brutally introduced into the mind-set of a sex offender, even though I was too young to realise the enormity of the crime of what had happened to me. Because of it, and other forms of abuse, mental, physical, and sexual can only be described as torture continued in every other place I went until my mum rescued us from the horrors of the Children's Welfare System. But it was not done with us yet. It had one more cruel hand to give us. But what were the horrors and were they really that or the imaginings of a disturbed, maladjusted, abused traumatised child. These were just a few of the adjectives used to describe me, these and pee—the—bed, pee pants and others, these are just a few small examples. Names may not hurt but reactions to them do, like having to hand wash your sheets every morning before breakfast and if you were unfortunate enough to drop them because you we're too small to reach the clothes rope then you had all of this to do again before you got anything to eat. Some people may think that if a child wets its bed then it should wash the sheets until you realise that the child is only four years old and under three feet tall. However, some of the children's homes were better than others, but not much and what usually made them better was, you did not always have to have a scalding bath until you almost fainted or get put into bath with a boy when you are reaching puberty. Although these incidents did occur, the difference was that it was not on a daily basis. The daily abuse would be silly things like being slapped for wetting yourself which then only made you wet yourself again, other small, but equally damaging little things was seeing all your visitors sweets being put into a bigger tin that was shared with all the children. If you didn't get one yourself and started to cry that was another slap for being greedy and selfish and to teach you a lesson to share and not keep all your sweets to yourself. For many of the children in care, life was tough and hard and the care staff was unqualified to look after lots of children with differing needs. A Two-year-old needs love and care not hardship and punishment for the least little demeanour. Then you have those reaching puberty that need guidance and support as they go through the turmoil of raging hormones, pubic hair relationships and shaving. Being allowed to develop as an individual with his or her own unique personality and opinion . . . However, that was not the ethos in those days. In what seemed very dark days the care system ethos seemed to be keep them fed and watered and clothed and that was about as much "care" that was put into the caring of the children's homes, Sometimes there was smiles as well as tears, or more to the truth, like matrons day off or the person in charge of the children gave them an extra hour up to watch the Eurovision Song contest or you would get an extra sweet by one of the kinder carer's because it was your birthday or you had managed to go a whole day without losing your hankie and yours socks were clean or for once your pants were dry instead of wet, or they were just feeling kind. On those days the homes were bearable and gave you enough happiness to last for a time no matter what needless to say I never did get a sweet because I either lost my hankie or wet my pants or my socks were absolutely filthy from playing in the muck. Birthdays were the worst. No matter what you got or who you got it from be it from your mother, sister or just a wee something from one of the other children it was needlessly immediately confiscated, and you really hated the matron or person in charge. Then when it was my seventh birthday this happened to me, I should say me, I lost all of my senses at once and shouted at the matron and then without hesitation kicked her in the shin as hard as I could, well I knew I was in for a hiding of a life time but I really didn't care. As far as I was concerned it was payback time. You can imagine the horror on the other children's little faces because I had broken every rule in what passed as a rulebook in that particular hellhole. She could kill me if she wanted to and I am sure she wanted too but she did the next best thing. She grabbed my hair and dragging me up the stairs not really giving a damn as to who saw or heard what she was doing. Missing steps and falling down, heels dragging behind me and by this time my shoes had tumbled back down the stair simply because of the rate she was literally pulling and dragging me up the stairs. What finally made me think I was in trouble was when she had asked two more staff to come with her.

The three staff then started using me as a punch ball they punched my face, my kidneys, which literally made me fall to the ground it was so painful then they kicked me senseless until I passed out. Now I knew what happened to you if you really stepped out of line and I had well overstepped the mark. After I came round with a bucket of cold water flung over me, the matron and her staff quite quietly asked if I had learned my lesson at which I could only nod unable to speak due to burst lips a bleeding nose and no doubt countless bruises she would put down to me falling down the stairs. The final punishment of the day was that I was put into the dark shuttered room with no clothes on and no sheets for 2 days, just to give me time to reflect on my actions. I knew by the punishment that I had just received that I was lucky. The next time I stepped out of line could literally be my last. Some of the happier moments that I remember with fondness are being in one children's home and although bonding with other children was difficult for everyone, I remember this one little girl in particular because she taught me some songs as we would both sit on the swings at the play hour before bed. She was slight in build and had short dark curly hair and freckles all over her I face and arms and the songs she taught me were

"I can sing a rainbow which goes like this:'

"red and yellow and orange and blue green and indigo a violet too I can sing a rainbow, sing a rainbow, sing a rainbow too, listen with your eyes listen with your eyes you will hear everything you see I can sing a rainbow sing a rainbow you can sing a rainbow too" . . .

I apologise for not remembering your name but I will always treasure "sing a rainbow" and the other song you taught me

"I once had a dear old mother who thought the world of me and when I was in trouble she sat me on her knee. One night as I was sleeping upon my feather bed the angels came from heaven and told me my mother was dead. So children obey you're parents and do as you are told for when you lose your mother you lose a heart of Gold."

Those songs and our time on the swings made life bearable in what was an inhospitable place God bless you freckle face, you made my life worth living.

Many of the early days were dark indeed, literally. For instance, when I had dysentery, I didn't know what it was but I was always covered in poo from head to toe and was put into isolation away from the other children in case I infected them and spread it round the whole home. How I contracted, it was a mystery to all. However I remember the word dysentery and it stuck in my mind because although I didn't know what it was or that I was about to find out exactly what happens when you have dysentery. As well as being left covered in my own faeces' I had no bed covers or nightdress and was left in a shuttered darkened locked room and the door and lights were operated from the outside with a key. The only time I saw daylight was to be given a scalding hot bath that left me looking liked a cooked lobster until I almost passed out, and then it was back to that dark rank room which was making me vomit into the bargain.

Other happier times included one of the hardest chores we had to do. Wax and polish all the floors, except the marble staircase, which we had to scrub with carbolic soap. This might seem a strange activity for younger children to be doing, but for most of us it was an opportunity to get out of schoolwork, which none of us was any use at or liked. The polishing of the floors became a regular chore of mine but I loved it. The big tin of orange bees wax was thick and solid and our small hands had to dig deep to get a bit onto a ragged piece of blanket. I can now, just thinking about it even smell that thick orangey waxy aroma. So there we were six of us between six and seven years of age, on our knees rubbing this lovely smelling orange wax into the real hardwood floor, bums in the air swaying in time to an invisible band. Whether it was the smell of the wax or the invisible band that kept our eyes averted from matron in case we were in some kind trouble or weren't polishing in the proper direction, whatever the reason we did not dare look at matron. That was the fear side of it, but the other side of that was that was the fun side when we got to run amok with blankets attached to our feet and were allowed to run, slide kneel and shuffle our way to what must have been the most highly polished floors In all the children's homes in Scotland. It was hard work but we made it fun and we loved being "volunteered" for cleaning the floors.

It is amazing the things you remember from childhood like the day our foster mum rescued us (Grace and me) from another children's home. At this point, we did not know about Marge although amazingly, we were only three miles away from each other, but at this point, nobody was making us any wiser to any sisters, brothers, cousins, aunts or uncles or parents for that matter which sadly were still about alive and kicking. By the time out foster mother recused us I was five and Grace was six.

In this particular children's home to summon all the children at once a big brass hand bell was rung and the children had to stand to attention with your feet touching the child next to you. If you were unfortunate enough to find your name being call you had to take a step forward, not knowing what punishment awaited you because half the time there was no "crime committed" to warrant the punishment.

Today it was Graces' and mines' time to face the music for whatever misdemeanour we may or may not have committed.

After our names had been called all the other children were dismissed to either get on with their chores or school work. As we stood there waiting to hear our fate or punishment a lady arrived in a fur coat with a diamond broach.

Much to our surprise this lady came up to us and asked if we wanted to spend the day with her, Tommy, Billy and Jenny. Grace replied immediately that she would like to. Then the lady came up to me and asked if I would also like to go with her however I was less trusting than my sister and just nodded. Not only did this lady arrive in a fur coat a bigger shock was in store for me. The car she had come in was massive. This lady must be a princess to arrive in such luxury. So what would a lady in a fur coat want with us, we were nothing but snotty nosed urchins and disturbed ones at that as the authorities had labelled us among other names. However putting my suspicions aside, I after getting into this massive car and driving away I started to ask about Tommy, Billy and Jenny, The names that this lady was always talking about and the more she talked about them, I was getting more and more excited to meet them. The questions I was asking were quite normal for a "disturbed "urchin. I wanted to know how long she had looked after Tommy and Billy and how old was Jenny? However I was beginning to get excited about the day out with this lady who looked after three other children, and who must be a princess because her house when we reached it looked as big as a castle to me. It turned out that her house was a large bungalow with a front and back lawn. The side of house had a beautiful rose garden and was full of rose bushes and standard roses. The front lawn was always perfect because it was cut, fed, irrigated, moss killed and other nasty weeds killed off with grass weed killer. However, the end secret as to why my mum's grass was in such good condition as well as all the feeding and cutting, it was cut, fed and watered by the green keeper of the bowling club, which you could see from the side of the house. If the grass was treated with this much TLC (tender loving care), then I was sure this lady would do the same for us.

I remember my first few word to her were that my name was Anne and Graces name was Susan but Grace was having none of it, her name was Grace and Grace it was going to stay

Grace asked the lady what she wanted us to call her. Grace wanted to call her mummy while I said no that aunties were much nicer than mummy's, which up until now had been my experience after a good few more visits I too wanted to call this lady mummy. Grace then asked if she could stay until she got married and our new mummy said that we could. What I hated in between these visits is that I had to go back to the children's home. As this new mummy nearly always gave us a bag of sweets, they were confiscated practically as soon as we got our coats off and put into a communal tin for all the children, and as usual, I inevitably never got one because of either wet pants or socks or a lost cotton hankie. That was not my first taste of injustice, there were many more before these sweetie incidents. Other people caused me to become very passionate about injustice and even now as an adult, I will fight fiercely against injustice.

As our visits became more frequent and longer, our mum asked us if we would like to be adopted. Grace says yes immediately, me, I was a bit more wary in that I thought adoption was some form of ownership and I didn't want anybody owning me. If my mum had taken the time to explain to me what adoption really meant I too would have jumped at the chance of being adopted instead of getting us moved on? From that day to this, I have always felt responsible for us being taken away from our foster mum all because I did not want to be adopted or in my young five year old disturbed mind owned rather than loved.

Although we both were taken away from our foster mother by the social worker with the little yellow beetle, which had the engine at the back and always made me sick I have never forgiven her for the way she carried out the move or the consequences of that move. We got moved during school hours. I remember being in primary 3 and was making a giraffe from pipe cleaners that were yellow when someone came into the classroom and said that the headmaster wanted to see me. Now when you are 7 years old and the headmaster wants to see you—you quickly march out of the class knowing everybody is staring at you because—whatever you have done must be very serious if the headmaster wants to see you. On arriving at the head masters office, I could hear this quite sobbing. It was my sister grace. I was soon joining her but anything but quietly. I wanted to see my mummy first. So did Grace. However we never got to see her and she never got to see us, although she had asked and pleaded too. In addition, what was worse she was given no answers or reasons as to why I too to this day do not know why we were being taken away. However, like I said I did not go quietly. I was screaming and kicking the social worker for what I was worth until they finally had to carry me to this, by now, hated yellow car, throw me in and lock the door. The social worker started up the engine and we moved to a place with an excellent reputation. Nevertheless, that reputation was only as good as the staff which runs it. The part we ended up in did nothing to alleviate my fears, cottage 13. You will like it here there are lots of houses with lots of children to play with and make friends with. With this statement still ringing in my ears as she shut the door behind her, she left with no further backward glance or reassurance.

In this particular home or village as it liked to be known was where the abuse was on a daily basis. Not only sexually but the torture that the cottage parent used to do to get you to behave or punish you by using wet towels to whip you with until you had weal's on your legs, back, and even covering your face when they were trying what felt like strangulation. In The cottage I started to cry for my mummy and that I didn't want to stay here I wanted to go home. Where at this point it was made clear to me that I could cry all I wanted because I was staying here and had better get used to it like all the other children in the house. Outwardly, I visibly wiped my tears but inwardly I was inconsolable. Here I was in yet another children's home forcefully taken from school with no reasons given and we never got to see our foster mum for a whole month. That month felt like a lifetime.

If you misbehaved there was a high price to pay. Staff, cottage parents in particular would wrap a steaming hot towel round your face and head and squeezed until; you stopped screaming or you passed out unconscious

Older children were often also used to abuse you in whatever way the cottage parent asked; in fear of whatever punishment they may be subject to themselves they carried out these abuses, although there were some who took great delight in subjecting younger children to abuse just for the hell of it.

This was a hellhole and I did not know what I had done to deserve it. Still classified as a pee the bed and still having to wash sheets in the morning before breakfast. I was sexually assaulted on a near daily basis by one of the older boys who went to the same school, which was in the grounds of the village. Then he used to get me at the swimming baths too and his threat unlike my "brother" in Lossiemouth, was that If I said to anybody about what he was doing to me, his reply would be that I'd asked him to do it. What defences did I have against that? None! Although not sexually abused by the cottage parents they had their own way of inflicting psychological damage, like putting down the same plate of vomited stew for three consecutive days at each meal and making me eat it until I would vomit it back up yet again. This would continue every meal and every day until I finally plucked up the courage to throw the plate of stew on the floor and smash the plate. No more, stew. However the punishment and the abuse continued. However the kickback to this is that even to this day I cannot bear either the smell of stew or the look and just cannot eat it without boaking and vomiting.

However, in among the horrors of daily living and abuse there was a time I got excited and that was Saturdays and Wednesdays. Why? Well on a Wednesday I would receive the Beezer and the Topper comics from my mum, but in the post to me and me alone, Grace got the Judy and the Bunty in her own little mail package too, and inside our mum had always managed to write us a letter each. As my reading wasn't as good as grace's she always read my letter to me. This little posted package made me feel so important and wanted and not forgotten about and made the abuse slightly more bearable. Saturdays were even more exciting because it was on Saturdays that our mum would visit in a car and we would go for a ride and a picnic. But the saddest part of Saturdays were that our mum had to go away again until the next Saturday. The big bag of sweets she left us was some consolation until it was taken off us and shared between all the remaining children. At some point and I really can't remember was that the home stopped my mum from coming to see me for 3 months to see if my behaviour would improve. Seemingly I was so upset every time my mother left that the authorities in their wisdom decided me not seeing her was the answer. Wrong, how very wrong this was to prove to be. I reverted back to my rocking and licking my lips I ended up spending those three months in what was called the Epilepsy Colony. I got sent back before my foster mother was due to start revisiting

What, for me summed up the place, was when I had anything physically wrong with me I can think of a few instances like when I was made to walk to the hospital within the grounds. It was a real hospital with real trained nurses and doctors.

Although it was small The worst case was when I fractured my knee playing football with myself, talk about falling over fresh air I can't even blame a bad tackle from an invisible opponent, and I was told that I was always complaining about something but if I wanted to see a doctor for what the cottage parent called a wee scratch I could make my own way up. By the time I got to the "Elise" as it was called, I was crying with pain then once the x-rays were taken I was horrified to discover that I had a fractured knee cap and was going to be in plaster of Paris from my foot to my hip and was being kept in for the six weeks the plaster was going to have to be kept on for. Those six weeks were the best six weeks I spent there. no cruelty from anyone in any shape, and I got to keep the bag of sweets my mother gave me but on this occasion I did not mind sharing them as there was only about another four children in the ward.

Other areas that highlighted the Victorian conditions were when I took worms, nits and scabies. The worm and nits I do not know how I got them I just did and boy was I made to suffer for it. A steel comb pulled roughly though my head every day and night. But I had to get medicine to treat the worms. However, the scabies I got from sleeping with Grace (that was when we were very close and she looked out for me. I slept with grace at every opportunity in the various children's homes but sometimes if I was caught you could be sure there was a punishment to fit the "crime" or not as the case maybe Contracting the scabies is caught through dirty sheets but when the doctor looked at us both, Grace was covered from Head to toe with tiny itchy red spots. I had a lot of spots too but only half as much as Grace, so what happened? The whole cottage was quarantined. And that was when they had the cheek to ask our mother to take us home until we were clear of spots and no longer infectious. Then once more, it was back to the home.

During our time at the village two things changed first Aunt Daisy (a family friend) who used to drive our mother to the various children's' homes to visit us, this stopped. Not the visits, but Aunt Daisy driving our mum, as if this wasn't bad enough suddenly "Uncle Jimmy "appeared on the scene, and he was doing the driving. Oh my Goodness!!! For a young child this was just too much to try to make sense of. This was, where, for me events were about to get much happier and once again my mother, along with "Uncle Jimmy" finally rescued us out of the care system for good or at least after they were married and came back from honeymoon.

There was nothing in this care system which was cruel, full of suffering and humiliation and did nothing that the word "care" implies. All I can hope for is that somehow, somewhere the law takes a lead and names and shames all the children's homes where abuse did and does, take place I am not that naive enough to think that it is wiped out. I also think that any legislation should be implemented and used in its strictest sense and should include foster care homes. For I believe that it still exists. But with strict recruiting and vetting procedures I can only hope and pray that things change dramatically homes are reviewed randomly by unannounced qualified officials and if there is proof of abuse of any sort there and then perpetrators should be charged accordingly and taken to court, and if it comes to it jailed.

In the sixties nobody listened to what the child had to say and if a child dare tell the truth the consequences were always met with a harsh punishment and left you with no, uncertain terms that telling it how it was, was not meant for outside ears and would only end up with further abuse. I think for me looking back at the children of the fifties and sixties, myself included we were not even aware that what was taking place on a regular if not daily basis was abuse or even wrong it was just part and parcel of being in a children's home. The abuse of power by the adults who could instil the fear of God into if, in their eye and it was their eyes only, you had committed some type of misdemeanour you would start crying just at the shouting out of your name. The sad part of it all was that we (the children) all thought that this was quite normal. How cruelty could delude you. However, the experience taught you very quickly that there was a hierarchy to that power, and that power was determined by the type, length (duration) and regularity and who was going to be the perpetrator. Because it was not always staff who would do the abusing. Older children soon became the bully with the same level of power and fear. The statement really echoed: the abused becomes the abuser although thankfully only a few fitted this profile.

Then one visit by my mother somehow made my life worthwhile. Uncle Jimmy was getting married to her and they were taking us out of the home after they got married. All the times of going to church three and sometimes four times a day made me actually believe that there was a God even a feared one and he had answered a little girl's prayers, even though she didn't really know how they worked, they just did. And my mother and "Uncle Jimmy were the proof of this. I could not contain myself and hoped that they would be getting married next week. As a child I had no comprehension to the time of things a week could be a month and a month could feel like a year. All I was concerned about was that I was leaving this hellhole for good and this made me love my mother even more.

After we came home uncle jimmy asked us to call him dad, which I did with delight. I was finally, at the age of twelve, getting a family of my own with my sister I finally had a mummy and a daddy it made all these hellholes small and insignificant and the one thing I knew for certain was that they were never going to be able to touch me again.

CHAPTER 3

The good years

My mums wedding day had arrived and mum was wearing a large beautiful jade and contrasting forest green rimmed mesh hat and a green jade coloured dress with two forest—green buttons on the shoulders and a similar trim of velvet on her hem. Although not a typical bride outfit, my mum still had all the radiance of a much younger bride. It needs to be pointed out at this juncture that my mother was 63 years of age, so she was taking a very brave step into the unknown. Her maid of honour was her lifelong friend Annie Wylie, who we called Aunt Annie. We weren't meant to be in the line-up or the photos—picture of wedding outfits on 2 girls—but me being me asked until my mum gave in. As I discovered years later there was a lot of surreal smiles that day.

For me the day was magical, for my mum and dad it must have been a nightmare knowing they had just made the biggest mistake of their lives and not only that but they had just married each other with no feeling for each other.

Although my Mother and Father had no feeling for each other, they both loved us to bits. My Dad and I got on really well. He took me to the coup to get rid of any rubbish and always gave me a wee shot at the car. Other incidences I remember with my dad were digging the foundation of the extension. I felt a real bob the builder.

After a few years of this sham of a marriage my mother eventually put my dad out. I was devastated because I hadn't had a clue as to what was going on. I just came home from school one day and my dad was gone. On this Basis I gave my mum an undeserved hard time. However all I could see was that she had thrown out the only father I had known. I am not going to air my mum and dad washing that's private and stays private

There were some funny times with my mum and one such example was that our mother had the attic converted in to a bedroom for us. All we had to do was keep it clean. Now to most folk keeping your bedroom clean mean keeping dirty clothes in a clothes bin and making your bed. Now my mums' Idea of cleaning your room especially if it's an attic is to sweep, mop polish dust and wash the skylight. All this was done while the hatch is up so that the dust doesn't come down the stair.

One weekend while cleaning I was desperate for the toilet now I am only about seven years old. There were only a few hurdles stopping me going. There was no toilet upstairs, the hatch was closed from down stairs and my mum couldn't hear me shouting on her because she was in her element hoovering. Dilemma or what! Then I had what I thought was a brainwave. Off to the side of the wall was a box room, now this box room was an Aladdin's cave, it had trunks of old clothes, boxes of shoes and hundreds of other things to tease the imagination of a young child. However, my immediate and pressing need was to find something to do the toilet in. The answer was staring straight at me, one of the shoeboxes. Therefore, I removed the shoes, the tissue paper and wee'd, and poo'd in the box put the lid back on it and shut the door on it. It was only a couple of days later, that are arriving back from school my mum asked us if we knew anything about this box which she proudly put in front of us. I do I piped up it was Tommy the cat. Well, our mother mused we must have the cleverest cat in the kingdom. Not only does he know how to open a shoes box and remove the tissue paper without ripping it, he also knows how to remove a pair of shoes, do the toilet and then put the lid on, yes we really to have a clever cat,

Right now that we have that little story out of the way who is the real culprit. I hung my head in shame and admitted to my mother that it was me who did the toilet in the shoebox. Only when my mum dug deeper on the incident and that I had tried very hard to get her to hear me but she couldn't because she was at the other side of the house hovering she saw the funny side of it and actually gave me a compliment at having the gumption to figure out to use a box.

This was to be one of many incidents and accidents that Tommy the cat was going to get the blame for. These incidents were not deliberate I was just I very backward and frightened child and an absolute natural at falling tripping breaking bones and getting into fights which was my way of defending myself. I didn't know anything else until I got out of the children's homes and was back staying with my mother Mary Ritchie. My mother had kept her promise—to take us home and out of the children's' homes we were in. after getting married to "Uncle Jimmy" and too me it was a present from heaven. For the meantime having two parents who actually loved me and me loving them back was not easy. However not loving anyone or learning to trust anyone for years because no one trusted us, which they displayed throughout continual abuse, was one of the hardest thing I have done. Although we were now technically safe and home I was happy although still full of trepidation as to see if uncle jimmy was going to follow in the path of all the other men he didn't and he wasn't and I absolutely adored him for it. For once in my young life I felt I was free, safe and loved and I have only two people to be thankful to my mum Mary Ritchie and my dad Jimmy Bardsley. They may have divorced a few short years later, but for me it was good while it lasted.

CHAPTER 4

Losing reality

As the summer wore on and I received my o'grades results I was devastated. I needed at least five good grade, o'grades to get into Dunfermline Physical Education College and I had failed all eight o' grades that I had sat and now my dreams of a future as a physical education teacher lay in tatters. I knew I had the ability but I now had the written evidence that I didn't have the brains that I needed to get into college. I had to rethink my options and fast. I knew one thing for certain I was not leaving school this year anyway. I applied to the police force, the army and nursing. I was thinking about jobs that would enhance my abilities. I did get an interview with the police force and I remember being mad at my mother for making me go in my school uniform. She thought it would make a good impression. However my interview lasted as long as it took me to take off my shoes which I did think was rather strange until the height rule came down to rest accusingly on my head at five feet two inches. I was then told that I was too small and to come back after I had grown those two miserable inches. I never did grow those two inches and today I am still five feet two inches.

My interview with the army didn't fare much better and again I was told to come back when I was seventeen and a half. By that time my life was unrecognisable to the one I had now and going back to the army became unfeasible.

I started to argue, become moody think everyone was against me, at one point I thought that I was invisible because nobody spoke to me or asked if I was alright. I started and to think that my family were conspiring to kill me, making plans when I wasn't home ignoring me when I was. My school days weren't any happier and I failed test after test and exam after exam. Nobody seemed too aware of my pangs of youth or what I was going through. Finally to add to it all the summer of '75 was to end up with me trying desperately to end my life.

As the summer continued my summer was about to come crashing down round about me. One day as I was working out in the garden weeding, my mum asked me to keep an eye out for the bin lorry so as she could get the garden rubbish out with the house hold rubbish (in the early seventies there were no such things as recycle bins it all went into a metal bin with a metal lid). As I was weeding the back garden

I never heard or saw the bin lorry due to two factors. One; there was a large lorry parked at the corner of my street and two; I just did not hear it. If I had heard, it which I hadn't, I would have let my mum know. What made matters worse for me was that a friend from up the road was talking to me at the gate at the same time. My mother then came to see if the lorry had been and I said no I hadn't heard or seen it. At this point my mum totally surprised me and I surprised myself. She called me a lair in front of my friend and then slapped my face. Before I could even think about it I had slapped my mother back, something I would never normally do. I then did what I did best I took off and ran.

   I had walked about a mile out of town when I started to thumb a lift from anyone who would stop. Again I was out of luck mainly because it was a nice summer day. After about an hour of walking and trying to get a lift finally a white ford van with two young men in it stopped and asked if I wanted a lift. I graciously accepted their offer as I was getting tired of walking and was glad of a seat. As time moved on the young men who would have been around twenty five to twenty eight asked me where I was going at which I replied "anywhere you want to drop me off". Again they asked me if there was anywhere I wanted to go. I replied "no" as I had run away from home. This answer was to change the consequences of the day and without sounding too melodramatic the course of my life for the next twenty years. You must be asking what on earth happened that day for it to have such dire consequences. This is what happened that day

   As we toured around in the van the men asked me if I would like some chips for my dinner as I might not get anything else to eat for a while. I was grateful of the offer as I had run away with no money or change of clothing or anything else in my panic. As I ate my chips in the font of the van with the men they suggested that as I was a runaway the police might be looking for me, so why not hide in the back of the van. Naively I took to the back of the van. After driving around, they stopped and joined me in the back of the van and I was not prepared for happened next. They started to unbuckle their belts and then their trousers. I was beginning to get scared and not without reason. They took it in turns to both rape me and then soddamised me. I had just been violated in the worst possible was any child teenager or woman could be. I was sixteen years old and didn't even have a boyfriend. Once again I was in shock. But I then thought they were going to kill me in case I could or would identify them. However my first thought was how I get out of this van alive. I did not have long to wait to find out. They both lifted me up by my arms and legs and literally threw me out and drove off. After landing on a dirt patch half naked and sore I just cried and cried. Then something glittering in the dirt caught my eye. It was a piece of glass and I sat there and for the first time but not to be my last I cut my arms with the glass. After I got up and got myself descent again I tried to run but was in too much pain, all I wanted to do was go home and have a bath and start to feel clean again. As I had no way of knowing where I was I spoke to the first person I met and asked where the nearest police station was. She did not know but pointed me in the direction of a female traffic warden. I know traffic wardens get a bad name but to me that day in August nineteen seventy five she was my angel and hero. I asked her if she could give me direction to the nearest police station and she did better than that she actually took me herself. When I got there I could not thank the traffic warden enough for her help and then she left. When I got to the police officers area I asked to speak to a female officer, and was distraught when there wasn't one in the building to talk to. I then asked if I could use their toilet and then my humiliation was complete. I had chocked the toilet with vomit and shit and then had to go and tell male officer of what I had done to their toilet. By the time I came out of the toilet a good twenty minutes later a police woman had been called in from the beat. All I could do was cry and say I wanted to go home. Then the questions started, how did I get here, did I accept a lift, how did my arms come to be cut would I go to the hospital to be examined at which I vehemently refused to do and started to cry even louder. When the police officers then asked me did I know where I was I had to reluctantly tell then that I hadn't a clue? The police finally gave up questioning me and at this point my continual crying was reduced to a quiet sob all I could do in way of response to the police officers questions was to hang my head in shame and either nod yes or no. The police officers gave me a comforting cup of coffee and gently bandaged my arms. As all I wanted to do was go home I gave the police my mother's telephone number and waited. And I had a long wait, not only was I in Paisley I had to wait until someone with a car could arrive to take me home. When Mr Stewart arrived the last thing I wanted was a long car journey with a man, but I had no choice. What I wasn't prepared for was the lecture I got all the way home about how much I had upset my mother. I often wonder if he would have given me such a hard time if he knew what I had just endured at the hands of two psychopaths on the journey home I as we were driving over the Erskine Bridge I asked Mr Stewart to stop the car. I was ready there and then to jump to my death off the bridge. Luckily for me Mr Stewart was quicker than me at getting out of the car and grabbed me and told me not to dare even think about it, I had caused enough trouble for one day. That only made matters worse as I got a further lecture all the way home as to how stupid it was and how selfish could I be? On arriving home sore and humiliated I gave my mum a big hug started to cry again and apologised. I didn't mean to hit het or to run away but I was scared after hitting her, at what she would do. My mum gave me a big cuddle back and also apologised for slapping me she was annoyed at missing the rubbish lorry. What I was not prepared for on arriving home were all the other people who were in the house. These were my social worker, my doctor, the police and Mr and Mrs Stewart. I was being threatened to be taken back into care and I was desperate to stay at home so readily agreed with the conditions. What nobody in that house knew that day was the terrible ordeal I had just been subjected to? I often think if I had said would things have turned out differently. I can only speculate. I finally got my bath and scrubbed myself internally with Dettol and the rest of me with a nail brush until my arms started to bleed again.

After I got out of the bath this incident was never spoken about again until I told the psychiatrist I was seeing in Argyle and Bute psychiatric hospital in Lochgilphead. It was too little too late. The rape had resulted in an unwanted pregnancy which was the reason for my first overdose this was intended to kill me and this horror child whom I thought was the devil child. Here I was a sixteen year old schoolgirl attending a psychiatrist and discovering I am four months pregnant. My life was shattered. I took my mothers' heart pills along with a bottle of surgical spirit. I got a terrible time at the general hospital I got my stomach pumped in. I lost the child and wanted this cocktail of pills and surgical spirit to kill me too. As you can see it didn't much to my horror. I asked my psychiatrist to tell my mother what had actually happened to me and why I had taken her heart pills and overdosed in the first place. However she never did and my mother and sister only found out about it five years ago. My mental state was getting worse. I took an overdose of my mother's blue heart pills and washed them down with surgical spirit. I was not taking any chances of staying alive. However I did but lost the baby. I always thought that the baby was a little boy, (and in 2010, with the help of rape crisis who were giving me support and counselling) I finally gave him a name and called him Luke. I bitterly regret having lost the baby now, but at that time I couldn't even have told you who the father was because both guys had a go at me. I could only see this baby as the devils child and I was carrying it. I was too terrified to tell my mother in case she threw me out and after the overdose the doctors at the hospital were giving me such a hard time for what they were effectively saying was that I killed my baby and could also have killed my mother by not leaving her with any heart pills. I had never left so lost and alone in my life and felt that every way I turned someone had it in for me. Even when my mother came to the hospital she too had a go at me with—that it was a really stupid thing to do, and what I was thinking of. But I can't blame my mother for thinking I was only attention seeking because she didn't know the full circumstances. I firmly believe had she known at the time like I believed she did from the psychiatrist, she would have been much more supportive and would likely have made me go to the police and tell them the truth. However that didn't happen. What would have happened to the baby I don't know as it was my mother only found out about the rape when she was ninety one and went to her grave not knowing about Luke and I am sure if she had known about Luke she would have found a way to help me look after him.

My life might not have taken the course it did what those bastards did as well as leaving me raw and bleeding they totally fucked up my head to the point that I was going to be become a prostitute. Mum you were worried about the wrong sister. I can't blame her for that, because she was totally unaware of the circumstances I had been through, because I never told her.

I always envied my sister she was very pretty and intelligent and always got the boyfriends, while I was very plain and sporty and even won, one or two trophies' and medals and was in every sports team that was available. I was the captain of the swimming team; badminton team. Hockey team first eleven, played tennis in the summer and joined Strathclyde Ladies Running Club, which met twice a week. But to join the best left you dancing on air. The best honour wasn't always winning but taking part, especially when you are only in second year and are asked by the physical education teacher to play with the fifth and sixth years, believe me they were fuming but I was ecstatic that the teacher thought that I was good enough to play with the seniors. I was soon accepted as part of the team when I started scoring goals representing the school at county sport level, and winning championships. Even when I won an award for academic excellence my mum never came to see me get the award.

The only bitter pill to all of this was that my mum never came to watch me play or collect my trophies and it was always a case of your dinner is in the oven and I was left to eat alone and I would cry silent tears at the family rejection that they showed no interest in my sports and wouldn't even wait to see or ask how I got on. Or spend the time to eat with me, which only added to my rejection and unworthiness. I was made feel a total failure because I had not passed one o-level, I had failed where my sister grace was a straight "A" student and I was a dunce. Having failed my exams and once again being called a dunce reminded me of the various times I started primary 1. In all the various schools that we went to and how I was nearly always in the dunces seat with the big witches hat with a BIG DUNCE written on it What didn't help me at school was that I was always being bullied because I was so stupid. This was because of a kickback to some of the children's homes we were in, in that I was always called backward, slow and disturbed. Well, all I can say is who is laughing now. I have a whole pile of" scotvec certificates" an HNC in print and print media and my crowning glory of academic achievement is three credits towards a degree from the open university. They are, Social Science Foundation course, biology brain and behaviour and introduction to psychology and health and disease. All of which

I am extremely proud of.—picture of graduation

Oh by the way did I mention that I self-published a book of my writings which consisted of three funny plays, a section of prose, a section of poetry and a final section of a few short stories. If anybody is interested the name of the book is called "MY JOURNEY TO FREEDOM" can be bought from me at a bargain prince of £4.50 + postage of £2.50 through my E-MAIL address which is *anne. Anneb2504@talktalk.net*

This book really broke the mould for me and gave me the courage and confidence to break through and out of the psychiatric care system which was to be for nearly most of my adult life.

CHAPTER 5

The Psychiatric Care System

My first naive introduction into the psychiatric system was in September 1975 at 4.30 after school. The doctor I saw said that he could not understand how I could not get on with my mother and originally put my illness down to teens, tantrums and tears. However he did continue to see me until December. However as we all know things do not remain the same for long. By now my mind was beginning to play me up. What were the things I was seeing and hearing was I going mad and did I look any different to other people, the way I saw myself change. What was happening to me. Why did I feel the devil was inside of me and why did I see devils and gorgons come out of the walls and hear them accuse me of stealing babies and murdering whoever was on the news that night? All I know is that I was scared out of my wits and did not feel able to tell anybody in case they just laughed and didn't believe me. Everywhere I turned the devil was there laughing and accusing and turning me insane which by now I was sure I was and thought that everybody else was sensing a change in me. By now I was becoming very suspicious of people, including family, teachers and pupils at my school. My doctor, at this point it was my GP who thought it would be a good idea if I went into hospital for a spell at which I immediately said no way. That December at home was terrible. My mum wasn't talking to me for whatever reason known only to her. My sister was in a mood, and I was left feeling undervalued and felt no more than a scullery maid as I was left to make the meals, wash the dishes while Grace and her children were treated like guests. So in my weird state of mind I thought that it must have been something to do with me and how I was behaving. Talking out loud and arguing with the television and scared to answer the phone or the door in case of abduction by aliens. However by the end of Christmas I took an overdose of asprin and coke a cola and this time I ended up in hospital again and this time the doctors again suggested that I go into hospital. Once more this was met again with a stern refusal from me, but with the strength of the Mental Health Act, 1960 he sectioned me under this act. To those of you who do not move around the mental health scene either as a patient or professional the "being under a section" means that you cannot leave the hospital until you have the express permission of your consultant psychiatrist? However psychiatric hospitals have unfortunate ways to keep patients quiet. Nor is it without its own forms of tortures and its own punishments. It gives you what can amount to a liquid cosh in a cup. Or as an intravenous injection, or a favourite form of control is by restricting your cigarettes. As a naive 16 Year old you don't take any that in and your mental state doesn't help either.

One of the things that I found strange in psychiatric hospitals is the way that you can find yourself at the end of the long arm of the law, and not even intentionally. You only have to be ill. You don't even need to commit a crime. UNDER THE MENTAL HEALTH ACT 1984 you can find yourself "sectioned", this is the long arm of the law. If you wish to appeal against that section you need to appeal to a tribunal. However under the MENTAL HEALTH ACT 1960 if you found yourself under a section you could only appeal to a sheriff. This is what I was being held under just for not being well. However I must admit, at this time I had tried to commit suicide and in 1974/5 it was against the law so I guess I did commit a crime, but one I was unaware of. This happened to me again when I was sixteen coming up for seventeen and I was working in a hotel.

I was not long out of hospital and while I was working in this particular hotel in Arrocher where the owner kept sexually harassing the female staff. There were only two of us because apparently he could not keep female staff and I wonder why that might be? Now as you might have guessed by now, I did not particularly take to his unwelcome advances and one night a few weeks later I once more became unwell mentally, not that I would have agreed, the Lord Mayor of London or the Queen herself could tell me I was ill and I would have still disagreed because you are not always aware you are ill. So you are not always the first to ask for help. This was the state that I was in. Fully clad in blouse and kilt I jumped into Loch Long not even realising that it was not Loch Ness and totally unaware of the dangers, I started to swim out and find Nessie the Loch Ness Monster. Not even realising that I was in the wrong loch, but totally unaware of the dangers I had not only put myself into, but everybody else that was trying to catch me who I thought was aliens. This might be the appropriate time to say quietly that I also had a meat cleaver in my hands. Now you are asking yourself what was I going to do with this meat cleaver, well looking back now I can see the funny side of the incident as well as the serious one. However at sixteen and mentally ill at the same time it was a deadly case of defending myself from aliens who I thought were going to abduct me and harm me. So the meat cleaver was thrown at all of these aliens. In reality the "aliens" were the headlights of all the cars that were passing that night and as you would rightly agree, the local constabulary were called and a big black mini bus arrived with all of these people who were trying to grab me. At this point all hell broke loose and I jumped back into the loch protesting my innocence and swam out as far as I could before three of these people jumped into loch as well and finally did manage to get a hold of me. It was at this point I started to fight with all my worth which wasn't a lot by now, but I put up a good fight shouting to these aliens or Martians or whatever planet they came from that I was calling the police on them they were not going to get the chance to abduct me. Then they said they were in fact the police and however much I screamed, shouted or fought with them, they threw me in the back of this big black van with blacked out windows which only served to heighten my fears for my safety, that and the fact that they were all dressed the same. When they finally got me in the van, still shouting and fighting, it was at this point and they sat on top of me to try and stop me from kicking them. My final destination that night was Dumbarton Police Station. My fears had been met these people whatever they were, took off all my wet clothes with a gentleness I could not understand and I immediately had fears of gang rape after the one I had so recently endured but they gave me a hot cup of tea and a blanket and said to try and get my head down and get some sleep. These aliens or whatever they were, were being nice to me. But why? My suspicions were raised which put me into a heightened state of anxiety. I could not figure out why these men were being so nice, was it a trick, or was it a trap? I just didn't know. The next day dawned and I was still unaware of my surroundings, still believing I was in an alien spaceship. However they had arrived at my mother's stating they were the police (which I didn't believe) and asked her for clothes for me. My mother then asked where I was and was told I was being held in the police station. After further questioning the police, my mother handed over clean dry clothes but she still wasn't allowed to come and see me. On returning to the police station these aliens then gave me clean dry clothes to put on unknowing to me that they had been to my mother's I didn't know how these clothes fitted me or where they had got them from. None the less I got dressed. Once again they gave me a cup of coffee they also gave me a bowl of cornflakes which I didn't eat because I didn't know what it was. After that we made a trip to the doctors' surgery where the doctor signed the dotted line of section papers along with my Social Worker of the time which put me into hospital on a detention order. I was taken back to the police station and was then transferred to the Argyle and Bute Hospital once again in a three car police escort. Four policemen In the first car, two police and me and my social worker who had also signed the dotted line in the second car, and in the third car, four more policemen. What a waste of resources. But then maybe they thought I was the alien. Who knows but it was off to the funny farm for the second time, otherwise known as Argyle and Bute Mental Hospital. On arriving at the hospital, which I did not immediately recognize I was met by three nurses and escorted to the locked ward. Now don't get me wrong here I have absolutely no disrespect to the other patient but the only thing we tended to have in common was that we were all locked up. An average age of the ward was about sixty five, which gave me no one to talk to. Here I was a young naïve seventeen year old and locked up in a loony bin. Some people may think I am being unduly harsh, but seventeen year olds should be out dancing and chancing their luck at the local pub and enjoying themselves not going to bed at six o'clock at night and up again at six o'clock in the morning. It was really weird in the summer watching the deer cross the grass while you're in the dormitory looking out the window. There were no curtains in those days, no railings, no privacy. Three rows of beds and stiff white starched sheets and a bright red hospital bed cover with the hospital logo all over it that you wouldn't even steal if you wanted too. At night time we came up in shifts in the lift from the downstairs day room, which had horrible plastic seats in it. One of the things I remember was the dining room it was noisy and packed and held about six different wards all having their meal at the same time. The drinks option at the time was a big pot of tea with milk and sugar already in it or a big pot of black tea which had left you with no options at all, it was a case of Hobson's' choice, take it or leave it. One of the times in the dayroom, I clearly remember sitting on a chair the next thing I knew I was getting scolding black tea poured over my head, because apparently this seat was someone else's which I didn't realise, by God did I scream. As soon as I stood up the person who had poured the tea over me sat down in the chair that I just vacated. She never got into trouble but I did for the racket I was making but then I'm sure if you got hot tea poured over your head you'd be making a racket too. All the staff kept saying was it couldn't possibly have been that sore but for days afterwards I couldn't brush or wash my hair or even touch my head it was so painful. The ward had big pillars at various points and was surrounded by lino which was polished twice a day by a ward maid otherwise knowing as the domestic. One of the other things that used to turn my stomach was when they bleached the cups the smell would make me feel sick almost every time. They would fill up a big metal sink and throw sterilizing fluid into the sink which smelled of bleach. This was done on a regular basis to keep the cups clean. The cups were made out of old fashioned plastic. Daily activities were carried out at the occupational therapy, this is where I first learned to knit socks and play chess also to my amazement I made a rug and a stool and my first Arran cardigan which led to many more. We got to the therapy by way of a bus this is because the occupational therapy building was in another part of the grounds and the reason we went in a bus was so that nobody went absent without official leave or went for a run on their own out with the grounds. We were counted out the ward and then counted in at the occupational therapy department. This was one of the few places you could actually mix with other patients from different wards. It was also one of the few places where you learned new skills and made new friendships, which wasn't easy. Occupational therapy took place twice a day, morning and afternoon and the whole routine would start up again the next day apart from the weekends where we would get a break. Depending on the weather we would go for an escorted walk. If we had a visitor which wasn't often because of the distance unless you were local you then got to go to the canteen with your visitors. The canteen served tea, coffee, biscuits, sold cigarettes and sweets. If you got parole you could go to the canteen as often as you liked depending on how much parole time you were aloud. This sounds like prison and sometimes it felt like it too. On occasion they would have entertainment in the assembly hall and the different wards would go. Some of the entertainment would be quite good and some of it crap.

Once a month the Salvation Army band would come and play hymns and entertain the patients. One time after listening to the Salvation Army, once I was back in the ward and taken up in the lift to the dormitory I took a sudden impulse to smash a window which I did and kept ripping my arms on it until they were bleeding. One of the cuts were so deep that my vein was showing and I got wrestled to the ground, jagged and taken away to another ward to get stitched and bandaged then back up to the ward again with two nurses watching me all night. This was to be the start of a pattern which got worse as I grew older, not only did I start cutting myself by whatever means I could for example Stanley knives, windows, razor blades but the voices and the demons didn't help. Hearing voices telling you that you are the devils daughter and the only way to get rid of them was to cut the devil out, to release it. This was to continue for many years and was not helped by the fact that I in my innocence trusted what I thought was a man of the cloth who ended up being a Satanist. How does a young girl cope with being told that she does in fact have the devil in her, and that this person who will remain unspoken from my lips, then went on to try and make me a sacrifice to the very devil he was so called trying to exorcise. Many reading this will find it really hard to comprehend, not least of all me. I trusted this person completely and was deceived in the worst possible way ever. I never really recovered from this incident for years, and not surprisingly I now have an inbuilt mistrust of people of the cloth, especially men.

This incident alone, as you might expect really knocked, not only me, but the whole hospital. It was kept under wraps if the person responsible left immediately which he did, never to return. But the fear never left. And I believed more than ever that because of this incident that I would never get the devil out of me. I was now even more intrinsically involved with the devil than ever before. And I was scared out of my wits. I would hear the devil talk to me and hear him laugh if I tried to tell him to fuck off I was not interested in what he had to say. To get him to literally stop for any length of time I would need either extra medication or held down by my hair or my short and curlies which was extremely painful and embarrassing, even more so when you then get either one or two jags stuck into you behind. This was never done without me struggling like the evil fiend that I was so sure I was. At other times I couldn't be more helpful. I felt like Jeckle and Hyde, two different people at different times. However my biggest mistake was that I was still scared to tell anybody because I still thought that they would think I was insane. I did not know or find out until much later that this is what the general public think of as split personality, or raving madman which in fact is very rare, however these symptoms are not as rare as people think. They are in fact symptoms of a serious psychotic mental illness, called schizophrenia. It is not a madness or insanity and definitely not badness but an illness, in some cases a very real life threatening illness, mostly too yourself but rarely other people. After about five admissions for trying to kill myself one way or another and with various psychotic diagnosis and further admissions to different psychiatric hospitals in the Glasgow area, my life followed this hazardous path for another three years, however it all ended in bloodshed after three years of trying to kill myself as I could not cope with the illness and the devil was getting the better of me. The voices took a far more sinister turn and started telling me to kill other people. This literally scared me shitless, because at that time I was in an open ward, which meant I could get access to what I carried all the time, given the chance, a knife. I pleaded and pleaded with the doctors to put me back to the locked ward, and all I was told was not to worry and given a pat on the head. The doctors did not even increase my medication. What happened next I neither condone nor make excuses for and that is something I need to live with for the rest of my life. I managed to get a knife and sadly and ashamedly I stabbed another patient. Only then did all hell break loose I was taken to a single room with six staff guarding me. After the incident I did go and get help for the patient before being taken away.

That night, immediately after I was taken away and put into a single room with just a bed, I was put into a straightjacket for the rest of my time there. What I do faintly remember of that night is that every time I tried to move, I got jagged with more and more medication. The police came the next day to take me away. However because I could hardly stand, the police handcuffed me to an officer at each side to help me stand. I was duly charged and put into a cell and promptly fell asleep not out of lack of appreciation of the seriousness of the crime I had committed but because of the sheer volume of medication I was given. The next few days passed in a bit of a blur. What I know for certain is, if had I been well or at least at myself and got the help I was asking for this incident would never have happened. My worst nightmare had just happened.

What lay ahead was an even worse environment a state mental hospital, without limit of time.

On arriving at the state hospital I was met with "here comes the devils daughter." and everything and everywhere you went was double locked.

When the doctor came to see me he said to have a good look round as I was going to be here for at least the next twenty five years. On top of these distressing remarks I kept my cool I was going to show this man, yes another power hungry man, that I was not going to be here for another twenty five years. I didn't show it but I was terrified of this, however it also made me determined to get out long before that. Here I was at nineteen years of age and looking at being locked up for at least twenty five years, even serial killers get less than that and I hadn't even killed anybody. Some people believe if you do the crime you do the time. I believe in this myself, and as I also said earlier I also believe in karma. And now is my payback time, through having major physical illnesses to deal with. I believe it is my punishment while my friends totally disagree. They say that God forgives all sin; unfortunately I won't find that out until I die. Until then, I'll keep believing he forgives me. However it will take a lifetime to forgive myself and I have to live with that, and so do the Doctors who reneged on their responsibility to a young girl pleading for help. As a sectioned patient at the time, that should have been the least that they could have done for me. A mental illness is a terrible thing, but sometimes the consequences are much worse as it sadly proved to be in this case.

Sometimes there are two victims in a case like this. Sadly I very much remorsefully and regrettably feel for the person I stabbed. Then of course there was me. I had at that time in my life, an illness I could not control or the doctors give the mixture of medication to keep it under control. My medication was changed many, many, times until I was finally controlled by what is called a depot. This is medication which is slowly released into the body by way of injection into the buttocks. The first depot I got was an anti-psychotic drug called depixal which I was given fortnightly; however, this was later to prove to be an ineffective drug for me, because it gathered in my stomach. This meant for me a minor operation to remove the lump that had gathered. This actually fell on the eve of Princess Diana's wedding to Prince Charles. I can tell you the firework display was terrific and the only way that I had actually seen the fireworks at all was because I was in Law hospital having this operation and for that reason only I was privileged enough to see them. Along with the four staff who watched my every move, the other reason I know I was the only patient from the state hospital was because you went to bed at eight o'clock and the rules never wavered. I remember the wedding clearly the next day and I could not help but think two things. The first thought I had was why would a good looking girl like Diana marry such an ugly dude as Charles? The second thought I had was O my God a lamb to the slaughter and in a much crushed wedding dress disaster. Was this an omen of what was to come in the years ahead? However I also had another thought too This new princess was going to be loved by the world over even more so after being in public the first few times

When Diana's son William was born there was such genuine rejoicing, as not a lot had happened within the royal family but now here was a royal wedding and now the birth of a son and heir to the throne all was well.

I made Prince William a pair of yellow bootees. I remember that I also made a pair of bootees for Prince Harry too when he was born.

Diana was to prove a lot of people wrong about motherhood and how she would cope with it. As it turned out Diana was a brilliant mum.

When Diana died in a car crash in a tunnel in France . . . . there was suspicion that she was murdered . . . . she was a legend. And today her two sons Prince William and Prince Harry carry on her charity work and good causes. The reason I go on so much about Princess Diana is because I was privileged enough to witness history unfold as it took place.

After seeing the doctor that morning I was discharged back to the hospital bent over like a hunch back. We had a special menu for the day, I can't remember what it was now but I just remember that it was special. Secretly I was happy to know that I was the only one that had been able to watch the fireworks the night before. The wedding was something that brought the country together even if you weren't a royalist. Sadly as it turned out Diana's death also brought the country together in a mass of national mourning. However her memory lives on to this day.

After a week I got my stitches out, believe me you need a steady hand for groin stiches and I can tell you I was certainly holding my breath that day. It was one of those times you were glad you were not a guy. The doctor came and cut them out and afterwards I was able to stand a bit better. After two weeks I was back to my normal self, as normal as I could be in a place like that. One thing the state hospital does for you is give you stability even if it's an unwanted one.

Making friends was very difficult and not encouraged however I did manage to make one friend and we got on really well. The staff used to try and figure out what we were I talking about. They thought we were making escape plans when in fact we were actually talking about the staff themselves. To resolve what they thought was a dangerous situation (in their minds only) they transferred my friend into the parole ward and left me in Alexandra. After summoning me into the office I got asked what we were planning, I came up with this bull shit story that I was planning to take the keys off one of the nurses, go and get the trampoline out the exercise hall, push the trampoline over the rutted fields to the high razor wire fence and jump over it. As a result of this cock and bull story which I literally made up on the spot I couldn't believe it when they actually believed my story and I got put into solitary confinement for nine months with no access and no mixing with any other patient. This itself had a very detrimental effect on me and I became very depressed and suicidal and tried to take my own life by ripping up my nightie and tried to strangle myself which didn't actually work but ended up me spending three days totally naked in a padded cell. Nothing to pee into but a gutter, nothing to lie on but a rubber floor, the door was double bolted, double locked and double doored so no one could hear you scream or shout or bang. I was injected every four hours with two injections, one in each bum cheek where one; it was very sore and two; unwarranted.

Most peoples' idea of a padded cell is white soft buttoned leather; however, the reality is hard black tire rubber with only a grill for ventilation, no clothes and far from soft.

For every time I was in the padded cell I had to stand up every day to a male nursing officer and I was totally naked, there was no way I could hide my modesty even if I tried or to cover myself. Then to hear those doors banging shut and bolted again was absolutely soul destroying.

On another occasion in a 'strong room' which is a room with a concrete floor, a hard nylon based covered mattress which was pulled out on a daily basis and cold water thrown in with a cloth and carbolic soap, for you to clean, and if the staff weren't happy you would get another bucket of cold water flung in. The only way to dry your room or more appropriately a cell was to ring out your cloth into your potty which was used to urinate in. One of my unsuccessful attempts to go on hunger strike ended in me having to drink my own urine because I had been denied water for over three days. I never thought that your own piss could taste as good as that cup did. I never went on hunger strike again.

On another occasion I managed to break a plastic spoon and swallow the handle with great difficulty, this was done in desperation to be taken seriously about the pain in my stomach. Unfortunately this back fired which resulted in me once more getting put back in to the padded cell. After coming out the padded cell I went to a strong room for six months solitary confinement and the pleasure of a cotton wool sandwich. This was literally as it says, two slices of bread with a large wad of cotton wool inside, and you were watched as you ate it so you would not spit it out. The spoon handle reappeared very painfully out of my rear end six months later black and as solid as the day I swallowed it

One of the weapons the staff used to use to control a patient was by controlling the amount of cigarettes they smoked. In a padded cell you got nil, in a strong room you got nil, in a room with a bed and a potty you got three a day. Once you managed to get out of 'C' corridor you were elevated to 'B' corridor which gave you a bed, a chair, chest of drawers and a potty and extra privileges. Privileges' were earned on good behavior and on a colour system, on this particular colour system you were on a colour for four weeks before being awarded the next colour but this was also at the staff discretion so you could actually find yourself on the same colour for weeks at a time. You could also find yourself going up or down this colour system depending on your behavior. The color red was 'C' corridor with no privileges and all you would do is scrub the corridor all day, once you reached the bottom it was back up to the top again. Staff would occasionally walk on the corridor and say you have missed a bit which would mean having to scrub the corridor all over again. Things got slightly better once you were promoted to 'B' corridor, mauve was the next color and gave you three cigarettes three times a day and no sharing or giving out cigarettes was allowed. If you shared your cigarettes with another patient you would be penalized and your cigarettes would be confiscated until staff decided to give you them back. On the colour green you got five cigarettes three times a day and on orange you got to go to the dances which unfortunately were not optional but compulsory so it didn't exactly feel like a privilege, and being the only females in the hospital we had to go to all the dances, whereas the men's wards rotated in turn. On orange, you got twenty cigarettes a day but to be on blue you were usually in 'A' corridor which meant you had a divan bed, a carpet, a chest of drawers, a comfortable chair and you were allowed either a radio or television in your room if you had one. I had a television only because I was studying with the Open University which I paid for entirely out of my own pocket. On yellow which was the top color, you were still aloud twenty cigarettes and were generally a house maid, kitchen maid or laundry maid. I was given an opportunity to work in them all. I actually believed this was because I was a trustee. Only much later in my life I discovered it wasn't because I was a trustee, I wasn't trusted an inch and the staff wanted to keep a much closer eye on me which was why I got kept on the ward doing these duties. Occupational therapy took place every day, both morning and afternoon except at the weekend when you got a break. The break from occupational therapy included, scrubbing all the corridors and washing the windows with the fire hose and thoroughly clean the dayrooms of which there were two. Also at the weekend in the afternoons of both Saturday and Sunday was visiting time. If you didn't have a visitor we would either watch the television or listen to music in the quiet room and smoke our cigarettes or eat a sweetie that your visitor had brought in to you from a previous visit or you had bought from the canteen.

Christmases' were always difficult and I remember I used to get a reasonable amount of presents but I also gave gifts to the other patients that didn't have any relatives and would therefor receive very few presents. To make up for this I used to buy five different presents to patients that didn't have any relatives or get any visitors. I did this not to be thanked but out of a general concern for the patient knowing that they would otherwise get nothing. You always got a large present from Santa which was from the hospital. At Christmas the meals were always special and you would get served by the staff, you would get tea and toast in the morning in your room and it was the only day of the year you got toast. You would actually take your time and savor every bite as you knew this was the only time you were going to get it. The staff actually let their hair down at Christmas; they would put music on and play games.

On the run up to Christmas I was usually asked to do the baking, I made toffee, tablet, fudge, Christmas cake and other delights. I remember my first attempt at making a clootie dumpling turned into dumpling soup. It smelled gorgeous but turned into liquid which was why I called it dumpling soup. My second try was successful it turned into a proper clootie dumpling.

On occasions if you misbehaved in the staffs eyes then about five or six nurses would grab a hold of you and pull your hair, grab you by the short and curlies and even on occasion would lay into me as in beat me up some folk may think I deserved it but I didn't do anything to anybody and still ended up getting a doing because it was their word against mine and your word wasn't going to get listened to because you were just a patient. On one occasion when trying to bang my head off the concrete floor it actually wasn't my hair they had a hold of it was one of the other nurses and they started banging her head off the floor until she shouted "it's me it's me" they only stopped when they realized it was a nurse and not me. Some people may think this behavior is acceptable however these people were meant to be trained nurses not thugs, although it was hard to tell the difference at times. Don't get me wrong some of the staff were really good to me but others could make your life a misery if they wanted to, and believe me they did. On occasion when a patient took a member of staff to court usually a male patient, it was always thrown out of court as the patient was always deemed to be an unreliable witness. I dread to think of the treatment that patient would receive afterwards. One of the things that really turned my stomach was when we all got a large beaker of salts for our bowels every

Saturday morning. This was in lumps, you had to chew it, and it literally made you sick. If this happened you were then given another beaker and if you didn't finish it you got another one. As you might imagine this absolutely ruined our innards, not only this but we all had to run for the toilet at the same time. The reason for this was that if you were "shiting you were not fighting". Given that there were only three toilets this made Saturday mornings a fighting field for a toilet with many of the girls having accidents with shit running down their legs, and I was no exception. What made Saturdays worse was that all the knickers you wore were comunnal. This meant that if you were very lucky you might manage to get a small pair of knickers to fit you or you may not. It all depended on how quickly you were dressed after your shower in the morning as to what size of pants you would get some days I was left with extra large pants that litterally kept falling down and that was just how it was. Menstrual period time was the worst as you were not given anything to hold your pad up with and this all predated stick ons and you were not allowed tampons of any discription. No tampax and no lillets it was worse if you happened to have your period while in a "strong room" or the padded cell you got nothing to wear at all. And the blood was left to run down your leg until you either got a wash or shower in the afternoon. While you got a shower every day you only got a bath on a Sunday and that was when you got clean clothes. While the men wore shitey brown uniforms the girls got to wear proper clothes but this was provided by the hospital store which was on the ward. Your allocation of clothes were issued to you on arrival and if didn't fit then the answer was basically tough. These issues of clothes were to do you until they either wore out or you grew fat on the medication and needed a bigger size. Nobody ever went down a size only ever up.

The stability the state hospital gave you was a false one because when it was time to be released or I should say discharged which in my case was decided by the Secretary of State for Scotland (at that time there was no Scottish Parliament) only he could let you out. In my case that was a very long eight years, although many of the women were out long before that. I believe my case was a political one. I had to be seen to do the appropriate length of time for the crime I committed even if I was well enough to be released years earlier.

The stability I was talking about earlier was actually mistaken institutionalization. With the same routine for eight years, no cars, no money, no social life to call your own, no friends, no boyfriends, although the women tried to have boyfriends but with no hand in hand allowed, no kissing, no cuddling, nothing was normal. We all adapted and buckled to the system and the system got everyone in the end. I always said to myself you may break my back but I am dammed sure not one of you will ever break my spirit. And they never did. They did come near on a few occasions but in the end I survived and in a place like the State hospital that is the best you can hope for.

On discharge from the State hospital, eight long hard years later and having lost my best friend to suicide on 2nd of January I was finally transferred on the 26th

March 1986 to the Royal Edinburgh hospital. I was originally put into an open ward after three days I phoned my social worker to take me back to the State Hospital; I just couldn't cope with outside life. Money had changed, traffic lights talked, cars were zooming past at a speeds I'd never seen before and out of desperation I pleaded to go back to the State hospital. My social worker at that time said my reaction was perfectly normal and just to give it time. He came to see me and told me everything was going to be fine and I was just to relax. Freedom didn't come easy. Other patients used to think I suffered from agoraphobia because I would not go out anywhere, this actually wasn't the case, the truth was, I was just too scared to go out. I used to go down to the reception, sit for half an hour and go back up to the ward. After a while the staff realized that this was what I was doing and started to make me go to Princess Street, which to me, was an absolute nightmare. I used to go to McDonalds', Wimpey or Burger King, have a coffee, take two sugars back as proof that I had been and go back to the ward in absolute tears. This carried on for a few weeks until one day the staff suggested I went shopping with them which terrified me. Once again we went to Princess Street. Before this outing I had walked to Princess Street from the hospital which one; gave me exercise and two gave me time to explore the surrounding area. However on this occasion this nurse suggested we go on a bus which I hadn't been on for more than eight years. I literally got on the door of the bus and back off again not even giving myself time to realize there were two different doors, one to go on and one to come off. Realizing my terror the nurse took me back to the ward. On another occasion one of the nurses took me to her home which we walked to which I was a lot more comfortable with. But I did not feel comfortable in her house and I kept asking to go back to the ward however she kept trying to reassure me it'll be fine and to just relax. She gave me a coffee in a China mug which I thought was so kind and a chocolate biscuit, nobody, at least not a nurse had done anything like this for me before. All this kindness however did not keep the demons away and soon they were back telling me to cut myself. I ran out of the ward, went to the local supermarket at the top of the hill, and got a packet of blades. Took out one, threw out the rest in a bin and proceeded to cut myself. I pulled my sleeves down but on arriving at the ward it was obvious that I done something because blood was dripping from my fingertips which were a sure give a way. However once I got stitched up I was put on 'specials' which meant I had a nurse beside me 24/7. Sadly this was not to be the last time I cut myself. As things deteriorated I went from trying to cut myself to trying to kill myself. This finally meant me going to the locked ward which unfortunately for me was full of very disturbed men and me the only female.

This lead to me being used as a punch ball by the men and also led to a lot of sexual harassment. On a few occasions one of the men would strip off all his clothes stand in front of me and ask me to dress him. Now I know the guy was ill but I wasn't exactly there for a holiday and I used to threaten this man, that if he continued to do this to me I would kick him so hard in the goolies that he would not know if he was a man or a woman. Luckily I never had to carry out my threat and even if it came down to it I don't think I could have done it anyway. Once again I find myself on 'specials' even in a locked ward. However even in a locked ward it is amazing how you can find spaces and things that you can harm yourself with. It was then decided, after a while, that I should go to a twenty four hour staffed social work supported hostel for people with mental health problems. On another admission one of my lifelong hobbies was emerging—photography. I still do this when and where I can and I even won a photography competition which was judged by the famous Jack Milroy of Francie and Josie fame. On first meeting my support worker (Ruth Buchanan) who was very skinny and had long hair, the first thing I said to her was she was an ageing hippy and I wanted nothing to do with her and her response to me was tough, you have me whether you like me or not. So after a couple of weeks I was discharged to Northumberland Street Hostel and as its name suggests was in Northumberland Street in Stockbridge near, the heart of town. Because I had been discharged from the State hospital on a conditional discharge which meant I could get sent back at any time if I misbehaved I had to have a social worker who was also a mental health officer and psychiatrist and could still do nothing without the permission of the secretary of state for Scotland. This was because even though I was not in hospital at this particular time I was still on a section which would see me returned to hospital a good few times more. Because of the various restrictions on me I was not allowed to go abroad on holiday or get married or get a job or stay out overnight at a friends' house.

Making friends was not easy and because of coming out of a régime that did everything to stop you making friends it was now equally hard on the outside if not harder.

One of my scarier moments came when my new social worker (Colin), Karen Rookwood (psychiatrist and Ruth (support worker) and me all got together to resolve a very serious situation which would have put me back into the State hospital by a simple phone call. However they stayed with me, talked it through and we finally resolved what could have been a very serious situation as I wanted to kill them before they killed me. I was becoming ill again and thought they were out to destroy me and I had to destroy them first. Lucky for me this incident was never reported to the secretary of State for Scotland and ended happily with no one getting hurt. It was a very tense emotional night. From it came a promise to talk about anything that may be bothering me and not to keep it to myself and not let these issues escalate to dangerous levels. I have to say at this point that Karen, Colin and Ruth were very good to me and believed in me when no one else did and for that I will always be grateful to have found three wonderful people who were ready to give me every chance possible to make a go of things.—First aid picture—One of the other golden achievements for me was when I won "student of the year" at first aid however, I totally misunderstood what the commandant had said when she said wear your best bib and tucker to the award ceremony and at this time I wasn't aware I was getting the award, only my first aid certificate so I was very emotional at receiving the best student award even if I was in a dress and jacket not uniform. Everyone else was in uniform except me; I was in a dress and jacket so I literally stood out like a sore thumb. After the ceremony Ruth had organized a party for me that I didn't know about either and she also tried to get me back with my ex-boyfriend which ended up as a total disaster. Although he was invited to the party he totally ignored me all night and played pool in the basement with the other residents. After that there was absolutely no chance we were getting back together. After the party I ended up crying all night only now that I am wiser I would never cry over a man again, but then, he was only the second boyfriend I had ever had. When the choice is either you or an imitation gun, most folk would choose the human but he chose the gun. After that, that was the point in no return. At one point I managed to get the gun off him and put it in a rubbish bin, he literally went ape shit because I had got rid of the gun and he said he would only get another one and that was enough for me. I walked away in total disgust, tears tripping that I had been given up for a gun. I hadn't seen him again until this party and the fact he just totally ignored me put the lid on it, it was definitely time to move on.

One of the good things about being a first aider was you got the various events, I covered shifts in the Usher Hall sometimes on my own which left me very nervous and was only too glad when a performance finished. Sometimes there was royalty there, sometimes there wasn't, sometimes there was even foreign royalty. The only down side was you never actually got to see a performance. I covered the tattoo for a good number of years, the first aiders were placed under the stands which was in my opinion was the worst possible place. If the stands had fallen down, the first aiders would have been the first ones killed. We wouldn't have stood a chance. One year I was actually in the Edinburgh Tattoo as a lady of the court. I was all dressed up in a wig, gown and cloak. It was the men that were guard's men and the woman courtiers and to get on the esplanade we walked between the pipe bands to get there. That year was fascinating and on the last night of the double house the soldiers would grab the ladies and bring them into the dancing reel. It was one of my most memorable years and it was so much fun. That was the year the Southern Gordon Highlanders were disbanded and I tried my upmost to steal one of their sweatshirts as a memento which was unsuccessful.

We used to go back to the barracks and get fed at midnight. By this point you were absolutely starving because you had been out by half past five and you arrived on a special bus with the soldiers and got taken back to the barrack with the soldiers. It was really quite an amazing feeling to be part of that. I have still to watch an Edinburgh Tattoo live because as a first aider, all you see is feet, when you are actually in it you don't see any of it, not even your part because you are actually doing it. My ambition is before I die to see a Tattoo. The year I was in the tattoo it was the seventy fifth anniversaries of the Southern Gordon Highlanders. I remember we all had to rehearse getting into a deer position and I was part of an antler and I have the poster to prove it.

While training as a first aider I was a very clumsy person and turned up every other week with a different injury on me and even a broken ankle. The rest of the first aiders used to laugh and say we know it's a first aid course Anne but you don't have to turn up as the casualty every week. I used to laugh along with them I could see the funny side. My highlight as a first aider came with the 1986 commonwealth games and we had twenty thousand children to look after. Many of them were measured for tracksuits and trainers during the Easter holidays and by the time the commonwealth games came in June, half of them had out grown their outfits. Their outfits were blue tracksuits, white tracksuits and red tracksuits which  represented the Union flag. On the way to the opening ceremony the children ran from Carlton Hill and down into Meadowbank Stadium, they ran into the stadium with each holding a flare and while they did that there was a fly past by the RAF tornados and the red arrows with the red, white and blue jet stream. It made an incredible sight. Looking after twenty thousand children was quite a stressful thing to do however after the opening ceremony we still had to look after them until twelve o'clock at night when special busses took them home at night to allocated schools where there parents would come and collect them. It was an incredible experience. Although we looked after the children at the opening ceremony, after that we had to look after all the public too, so there were a lot of people to be catered for and if you didn't have your pass on you, you didn't get in. I covered events at the commonwealth pool, covered other track and field events at Meadowbank Stadium and others that I can't remember off hand but I would do in

 an instant all over again. I still have my commemorative medal to this day which actually encouraged me to take up my running again. I did a couple of 10k's and 5k's and a 6k called 'I ran the world' I applied to do the Glasgow marathon but the staff wouldn't let me as I was in hospital at the time and it would mean someone would have to run along with me. Plus I couldn't afford the entry fee as I was only on £7 a week benefit money.

My years as a first aider in Edinburgh and the friends I made of Ruth, Karen and Colin made my life worthwhile even when I didn't want it too.

On another admission to hospital I was desperately suicidal; once again I ended up in the locked ward but this time not on specials. I managed to rip my sheet up into a strand and put it in my pocket I then casually walked to the bathroom, closed the door because on a locked ward the doors didn't lock and tied the sheet round my neck then round the pipes and jumped. Before doing any of this I phoned Ruth to say goodbye which in actual fact saved my life which I hated her for at that time. On being cut down I was unconscious and taken to a single room and came to with a nurse rattling on about God and how it was his decision how, where, and when I died, not mine. The reason I got cut down was because Ruth phoned up saying I was going to do something which alerted staff. For a while I never forgave Ruth for this because at that time I saw no way forward and no light at the end of the tunnel. After this it was decided I was to move on to Albany Street which literally broke my heart. I had become very close to Colin, Karen and Ruth However Colin remained my social worker and Karen remained my psychiatrist but I had to let go of Ruth. Albany Street was not a nice place to be in. It was a hostel for people with criminal backgrounds and addicts who stole to feed their habits. Meals were made by the residents and being a vegetarian at that time no one catered for me and when it came to their turn to make a meal I was always left to cook for myself and everybody else but no one catered for me when it was their turn to make the meal. I made friends with one of the girls in the hostel who had, like me, mental health problems but she was very naïve. At one point it literally was three men and a baby when she found out she was pregnant although it turned out she had twins. While she was pregnant all three men wanted to marry her but it was me that went to all the scans and was her birthing partner. It was an absolute amazing experience watching the twins being born. She only had a five hour labour. Unfortunately she ended up with post-natal depression and ended up back in hospital with the twins. We kept in touch for a long time but after I moved back to Dumbarton I lost touch with her and the twins. After moving out of Albany Street I got my first supported house by the Edinburgh Association for mental health. It was a shared apartment. At first my new flat mate was terrified of me because I had come out the State hospital and she said she didn't want to live there with me because of that. However she changed her mind. We spent our first night together on chairs pulled together because we had no beds. The beds arrived the next day and we chose our rooms. I had the one at the front and my roommate had the one at the back. We shared the bills we had three different tins and put ten pounds in each tin every week. One tin for phone bills, one for rent and one for electric. This covered all our household bills which left us with approximately ten pound a week for extras once our rent and poll tax was paid. While there, I started looking for jobs and started off working with the council. I had been on a scheme that gave you ten pounds on top of your benefit which I used for driving lessons. I took lessons for a year before sitting my test which I passed first time round. This enabled me to get a job with a car. My first job was with Edinburgh District Council as a clarkess in the planning department which covered private houses, road works, repairs, digging up the road by gas board, electricity board and water board. My job was to file all the planning applications and get them all ready to go to the planning meeting. While in this job, I applied for a job with the Scottish Association for Mental Health as a national advocacy worker. My interview included a written presentation of five thousand words, you were asked to leave at this point while they read your report then they asked you back in half an hour later to answer questions on your report and how you would do the job. This job was the highlight of my career. It included going round all Scottish psychiatric hospitals, setting up a patients' council and trying to get the hospital management to see the benefits of this. I wrote a report and a book called 'advocacy—a user's guide' which at the time was referred to as the bible and gave a lot of people their first insights into the different types of advocacy. This job I thoroughly enjoyed. Sadly only lasted eighteen months to two years then I ended up back in hospital and then was asked to take a year out. I didn't want a year out but I had no option. When I came back after a year my job was gone, I had a new job description I was no longer a national worker, and I was demoted to being a regional one. My new job was now user involvement and how service users could become involved in projects whether local, regional or national. I continued training nurses, managers, project workers and users themselves in how they could get involved. I spoke at conferences, spoke at workshops until once again I was made redundant. My job was gone. I did however have time to get another job but received no redundancy money. My next job was with a disability organization which again I thoroughly enjoyed but got made redundant after six months. One good thing about the jobs I had was it enabled me to work with adults with learning difficulties to set up their own councils within their day centers. Unfortunately this came to an abrupt end due to the introduction of social inclusion. Once again I found myself unemployed.

After about five years in supported housing I finally moved into my own house which was not supported but was a housing association house. At this point in time my Mother's health started to deteriorate and I started to commute from Edinburgh to Dumbarton for the next year. I finally made the heart wrenching decision to leave my friends and move back to Dumbarton permanently to look after my mother.

Mother and I didn't always appreciate each other's company and sometimes she didn't appreciate all the help I gave her. My mother was a very proud lady and did not accept help easily. At this time I was given a Community Psychiatric Nurse (C.P.N) by the GP's practice that I signed up with. I don't think my mother took kindly to this, I think she tried to understand what was going on for me but couldn't fully grasp the situation and I think she was annoyed by the intrusion of a C.P.N. and it highlighted for my mother that I too had something wrong with me. While staying with my mother, I got a house in Bellsmyre in Dumbarton and I stayed there for a year, going down every day to see my mother and at night when she needed me. Sometimes this was quite stressful for me as I had to deal with my own problems as well as my mothers. This led at times to admissions to Christie ward which was the local psychiatric ward within the Vale of Leven District General Hospital. On occasion I would be transferred to the Intensive Psychiatric Care Unit (I.P.C.U) generally for hurting myself and after a few months I would be transferred back down to Christie. What was different about the I.P.C.U. was one; it was a locked ward and everybody had a single room and nine times out of ten there were more men than women but I was no longer a punch bag for the men and I did not get sexually harassed either. Eventually the staff got to know me in I.P.C.U. and Christie ward, as once again my illness took hold. At this point in time and I am now fifty three I have not been in a psychiatric ward for three years. One of the last times I was in hospital was during my fiftieth birthday. The staff allowed me to have a small party in my room in the afternoon, where Maggie my best friend and others came to see me. Maggie brought my dog Bailey who was a Shiatsu to see me. It was great to see him because due to my ataxia I could no longer look after him properly and had to give him up. I was lucky that Maggie's brother Willie was happy to pay me what I paid for Bailey. At the time I gave Bailey up he was only six months old. So he had every chance of settling in with his new owners. Willie and Tricia gave baily a good life and sadly the wee soul had to be put down in April this year. He was only four years old, but I know Tricia and Willie, her husband, gave him every chance. God bless you bailey and may you be jumping up and down, chasing balls and having endless walks like the ones that Tricia used to take you on, in doggie heaven.

My last admission to I.P.C.U. included me slashing my stomach wide open to let the devil out as I thought. This resulted in me getting rushed to Paisley Royal Alexandra hospital and getting forty staples inserted without a local anesthetic which I am sure was done out of badness and not kindness to teach me a lesson not to do anything as stupid again. After a further prolonged visit to the I.P.C.U. in the Argyle and Bute hospital, I can now hold my head up high and with pride and apart from a three week respite period I have not been in hospital for three years. It has been a very long road and a very painful one at times. On one of my admissions to hospital and quite an early one to Christie ward in the Vale of Leven hospital it was suggested that I attend a day hospital for people with severe and enduring mental health problems. The day hospital was called the Clyde unit and was staffed by nurses, occupational therapists and over the years that I was there the unit went through a number of them. I started going to the unit as the patients used to call it from the ward on Tuesdays at first then Tuesdays and Thursdays. This is where I met Maggie who was to become my best friend, although I did not met Maggie for a

while as she went on different days to me. Eventually we met and hit it off instantly after she asked me to sit beside her. After five long lonely years I finally had a friend. Moving my seat to sit beside Maggie was the best moves I ever made as she became a very close and dear best friend. At that time all, those years ago, I didn't realize just how much of a friend Maggie was going to be. We are now inseparable. Maggie and Ruth are both my best friends. Ruth is the logical and serious one while Maggie has a lot of common sense and advice and she will defend me to the hilt and me of her, we speak to each other every day at least three or four times and phone each other every night to say good night. We even printed out and signed adoption papers, adopting each other as sisters. You cannot get much more commitment than that.

At one point Maggie and I went on holiday with each other and we went to Austria. We had the time of our lives however before we left Maggie was in shorts t-shirt and a baseball cap, I was in trousers and a jacket. My mum was absolutely aghast at what Maggie was wearing and thought Maggie should have got dressed for the occasion however Maggie thought she was appropriately dressed for going on a bus as we had all the way to go to Southampton to get the ferry over to France. On arriving in Austria we were met by snow but our room had a balcony which was great although the food was something to be desired and was also an acquired taste. The day trips we went on were good, although no one on the bus liked to courier, because she didn't help anybody and when people were sick due to the motion of the bus, she charged them a euro for a bottle of water and didn't even give them a sick bag.

At one point during our stay, an outbreak of diarrhea and sickness swept through the hotel we stayed in and it was quite funny because the men kept coming to our room and asking me for my incontinence pads and if we had any Imodium which I thought was quite funny. As a result of giving out pads and pills, by the time Maggie and I took it which was the last day of the holiday we had no Imodium left for us, only pads. We were both as sick as dogs with nothing more to puke into than a paper bag. When the courier left the bus at France we all gave an almighty cheer and when the driver took over and we were all delighted. It was a memorable holiday but sadly Maggie and I haven't managed to get away anywhere properly since. Maggie and I are like an old couple, we fight, we argue but we always make up. The arguments are usually friendly and never too serious, just good banter between us.

Since my mother died in 2007 Maggie has had me at her house every Christmas. This was more that my own family did for me. They didn't even ask if I had somewhere to go, If it hadn't been for Willie and Maggie asking me for Christmas dinner and offering me a bed I would have spent my first Christmas after my mum' death on my own. Maggie came to my rescue and I have been going there ever since. God bless you Maggie you really are a true friend, and you know you are always trying to kick my big proverbial bum here's your big chance

KISS MY ASS

I have had Claire as my Community Psychiatric Nurse (C.P.N.) for a number of years now and we get on really well. She has helped me through a lot and seen me through a lot and I have a lot to thank Claire for. Claire was not my first C.P.N. My first nurse was Gerry then Claire then Dorothy, Shirley-Anne I think it was then Jackie then back to Claire I have a lot to thank them all for. The one person I haven't mentioned yet is Ross. Ross did a lot of cognitive behavioral therapy with me, which, nearly always left me in tears and feeling shit about myself which it is supposed to challenge. In the end we called it a day.

While I was on another admission it was decided that I would go to what are called "the cottages" which are part of the Argyle and Bute hospital. The cottages main purpose was and is rehabilitation and though a lot of the patients were long term I was to be there initially for six months. However while at home for Christmas and New Year my mother took a terrible fall in the bathroom. When she collapsed, she banged her head against the door frame and then fell backward with her back getting hit badly off the wall. It was only discovered over nine months later when my mother was diagnosed with breast cancer and was going for a pre-assessment before having a mastectomy that she had in fact broken her back in three different places from the fall at New Year. The really sad thing about the mastectomy was that it was my mothers' second, and that affected her quite badly, and as a result when the district nurse left, I was the only one that was allowed to give her a shower. Even when I was in hospital I had to give the staff some cock and bull story about going shopping or going to the cinema or a very long walk, anything just to get off the ward to give my mum a shower. I wasn't complaining, it got me off the ward and brought me and my mum closer. But for the time that the district nurse was giving my mum her shower I had to strip her bed to the base, now my mum did not believe in duvets, it was a blanket on the base, then the electric blanket on top of the blanket, then a protective cover on top of that, then finally the bottom sheet. That was just the bottom half of the bed you should have seen what went on top. First there was the sheet, then two woolen blankets, a seer sucker cover on top and finally a satin bedspread. This all had to be done in the space of five minutes because that was how long it took the nurse to shower my mum. Believe me it was like an Olympic event trying to get this bed made in the space of five minutes. Between stripping it down and making it up and it all had to be done in hospital corners, I was exhausted by the time I was finished. After a while you got used to it and I managed to get quicker and quicker at it which for me was quite an achievement. After I started showering my mother she used to really enjoy just sitting there letting the water run all over her, especially her feet in cold water, so she could actually enjoy it much longer than five minutes. If my mum could have got away with it, she would have spent an hour in the shower I had to try and restrict her to at least half an hour but she nearly always got the hour she was after. If she got cold I just re ran the hot water all over her. After she had her shower I used to have to really rub her dry, put talc all over her, put on a clean nightie and put curlers in her hair and dry her hair with a hairdryer. This all took in total about two hours.

One of the projects I was on was at Kelvindale which took place in the grounds of Gartnavel Hospital. It was a printing project which taught me some basic computer skills and the essentials of printing which actually encouraged me to go onto college and do my HNC in print and print media. I was the only female in the class, and took a lot of ribbing but what really pissed me off was when a couple of the boys deleted my work for the hell of it and were only given a warning and I had to do it all again. However I did pass the exam and I am now a proud owner of a HNC certificate. I didn't go on and do a HND because that was going on about the management side of printing and I wasn't into that, I wanted to continue my experience with machines. However that never materialized either and I ended up back in hospital. I loved doing the print and doing the print media and would have absolutely loved a job in printing but this was not to be either. All this happened before I went to the Clyde unit which is now run by Richmond Fellowship which is a mental health organization. Previous to Richmond Fellowship I had a support worker from Scottish Association of Mental Health (SAMH) which basically meant I had come full circle. From working in a project with SAMH way back in 1987, working for them as an advocacy worker and user involvement officer, I was now back as a client with a support worker. These changed periodically and this carried on until the council introduced charges for your support. Because I started paying fifty pounds a week and the days I had two workers to take me out in my wheelchair I was charged one hundred pounds a week. This as you might expect led me to give up the service but I continue to go to their supported groups, a woman's group on a Wednesday and a drop-in on Saturdays. It seemed as my mental health improved my physical health deteriorated and being in a lot of pain does often depress me. Due to the continual pain I have been back in hospital due to depression over it. I have a degenerative neurological condition which will eventually see me permanently in a wheelchair. I also have fibromyalgia which is a very painful arthritic condition and means getting steroid injections every so often which as a result leaves me fat and unhappy at my weight even though I eat as healthily as I can I am still obese which really upsets me and I find hard to cope with.

Karen is my new support which I pay for privately; she helps with my finances too which is great. Up until Karen took over I had little or nothing in the bank, due to Karen's prudence I now have a healthy bank account. Having moved house helped because I was no longer near shops and I could not spend all my money on whatever took my fancy that day. I did spend far too much on clothes and now have a prudent wardrobe instead of a bursting at the seams one. Due to Karen's careful watching of money I now only spend money only on the things I need. Karen is a great help and takes me out socially and helps me with any other worries or issues I may have. Fiona was with me for under a year and did much the same things. I may have decided to let Fiona go but we did have some laughs and still remain friends. I remember going for a photo shoot of wild deer and we were stand about the Green Wellie Shop and as it was cold we thought we would take some pictures of the landscape.

I took a few of the landscape then decided why not have pictures of each other to remember the day. Wrong move!, because of the ataxia that I have and the fibromyalgia which at this point in time had not been diagnosed I could only move my arms so far and then I would double up in agony. Just as I was about to come down the slope to take Fiona's photo I could not stop myself going down on momentum. As I got faster down the slope I thought that I could stop by running into the car however I missed the car by a mile and ended up face down in the concrete and stones. The end result was that I continued on with the photo shoot and got some really good pictures of both stags and does and fawns. However the next day I had two wonderful black eyes that lasted about two weeks. I did see the funny side and fortunately for me nobody thought to take a picture of me while in that state.

In 2006 my mother was taken into hospital with a chest infection. This had been going on for some time. On the day she was due to be discharged from the hospital (March 2007) she took a very bad stroke and almost immediately she went into some kind of dementia. This was to last until she died a week later of pneumonia. I was with her right until the end. I contacted my sister and nephews and once they had arrived I gave them all time they wanted to be alone with my mother. I had said to my sister that I had to go and get my medication, she didn't want me to go but I had too much medication to take to miss. I told her that I was there for the long haul and just as I was going out of the room I was sure I heard what some people call the death rattle but I wasn't sure. By the time I had returned my mum was gone. I ran up the corridor to her room but I was too late she had gone. I just cried and cried then my sister Grace and me hugged each other trying to give each other some comfort in the face of immediate death and shared loss. Then I had this really stupid thought I'm an orphan and for the second time. After the death of my mum it was business all the way giving me no time to grieve.

First I had to register her death and then arrange my mum's funeral. I found all of this really daunting but I was given helping hands by Grace and her family and Mary Grayham. Thank you all immensely, I couldn't have managed it on my own. I think for me the worst part was choosing a coffin and the thought of the funeral itself. On the day of her funeral we all met at my house, as we waited for the cars to arrive the budgie we had at that time actually managed for the first time to finish the nursery rhyme Gorgie porgie pudding and pie . . . while he was under a cover. It was like his farewell to my mother. At my mothers' funeral I read out a couple of poems that I had written, not particularly for her funeral but just how I felt and what my mum had meant to me. As I believe in angels I totally believe she is back in heaven with God and her Guardian Angel. It was my small tribute to my mother. Her funeral was a dignified service with all her favorite hymns sung in her honour. I could not hold back the tears when The Old Rugged Cross was played The minister said some wonderful things about my mother and as the service progressed I could not hold the tears in check and once again the tears flowed down my face; she signed up for the R.A.F.: Mum had fostered us. And many more facts and complements like that. After the funeral at the church, it was on to the crematorium. This part of the service really affected Grace badly and she could not control her crying which in turn set me off. But funerals are sad occasions', even more so when it is one of your own loved ones. The meal afterwards was held in the Abbotsford hotel where she had also spent an afternoon tea celebrating her seventieth birthday. When my mum died on March 14th 2007 a large part of me went with her. Her ashes are now interred at her family plot in Dumbarton cemetery and I visit when I can. I remember clearly one of the things that my mum used to say about flowers and it has stood me in good stead since, give flowers to the living and don't wait till there dead. However the people I now want to give flowers to keep telling me to buy them for myself, so I do, but due to this statement alone, I used to buy my mum a bunch of carnations every week with the shopping. Sadly I never got any back. At the time I buried my mother I also gained my freedom. This may seem a harsh thing to say, but after looking after my mum for the last ten years before her death 24/7 I was exhausted. Unfortunately for me by August 2008 my legs were beginning to go weak and at one point I could not stand up or walk. After five weeks in hospital I was finally diagnosed with cerebellar ataxia which I contracted through a virus in my spinal column. There is no known cure at the present time but research is always coming up with new ideas. It is degenerative in nature and I will at some point in my life get worse until I need 24 hour care, hopefully in my own home. More and more services are getting geared up for home care. I never thought I would see the day where I would need homecare myself. However due to my various physical conditions I now have I get home care four times a day and seven days a week. This enables me and helps me to gain my independence which I totally appreciate.

At this point I cannot miss out little Erin who has been a great help in getting this book up and running and keeping it going. She has typed, and a lot faster than me, while I have done the dictating and majority of the typing of this book.

Talking about books as I have mentioned earlier due to my mother generosity I managed to get my first book printed the only sad part of the launch of it was that my mother was not there to see the end result, if you are looking down mum thanks for the help to print my last book and publish this book.

There are many reasons I consider myself as a survivor, mainly due to many of the abuses suffered as a child, learning to trust again, learning to cope again and learning to love again, all of which I thought I would never be able to do. I have many people to thank for this, rape crisis counselors, in care survivors Scotland counselor Sandra, who saw me through telling my story about Quarriers. Sandra counseled me for quite a while through various abuses. Other people who helped me are Maggie, Ruth, Colin, Karen, Karen and wee Erin who helped type the book, all I can do is give you all a huge big thank you.

I would not be here today if it hadn't been for all of you and all your hard work and it is all of you who have made me a true survivor. I faced my demons and won and that makes me a survivor.

Most people look down on me because of my scars on my arms and belly, I can tell you one thing if. it hadn't been for these scars I would have never have survived. One thing I am and always will be is a fighter and survivor.

For those of you who have either faced demons of abuse or mental health I hope this book has given you some sort of hope for the future. Because if I can face my demons which have plagued me all my life and overcome them with both professional help and help of my friends, and rape crisis, in-care survivors Scotland and others, then I can only encourage you to make every effort to either seek counseling or professional help from health or other services. All I ask is to try.

One of the things that I have learned after losing all of my work four times in a row and having to start all over again was that it wasn't only time consuming, or even tedious, frustrating, yes, but one of the things that you do not prepare yourself for is that you go through the trauma four different times. You relive the moment you are at in the book and at times that can be terrifying. Not only that but the knock on effect that has on other people. Using health services again or thinking that you have gotten over your demons and finding out it then blows up in your face. I know that this book was meant to be written because if not I would not have continued to put myself through all the gamut of human emotions possible. You feel sad, then happy, then angry, then smile, then feel insecure or frightened. In the end you go with the flow and follow it to where it takes you. Whoa and behold before you even realize it you are at the end of you journey.

Take it from me where there is a will there is a way. It will be hard and difficult but worth the journey. Only you will know when you are ready to take to take those first tentative steps; I wish you every success in your journey to wherever it leads you.

All I can say is to anybody who has been or is in my situation please find someone to talk to whether a professional or health visitor or whoever they may be, and through this you too will come to your journeys end wherever that is. And you might actually surprise yourself at how well you are actually doing. It might not be as bad as you think . . . I shall be thinking of you and wish you well.

This book is ending off where it began with a visit to Canada and my niece Debs' wedding to Stefan. Now it doesn't come much better than that, although after having two stroke's, I do not think the medics in this country will allow or insure me to fly but I can only try and I do that quite well. My final word is, I should not be alive but I am and many people frown on or shy away from me because of my mental health problems and my scars. These scars make me what I am, a survivor. I will continue to survive as I take my first step on my next journey to wherever it leads,

The end

Printed in Great Britain
by Amazon.co.uk, Ltd.,
Marston Gate.